Regional Stories of India

LINTHOI NINGTHOUJAM
MADHUMITA GUPTA
SARABJEET GARCHA

ILLUSTRATIONS BY
CHANDRIMA CHATTERJEE

SCHOLASTIC
New York Toronto London Auckland
Sydney New Delhi Hong Kong

Published by Scholastic India Pvt. Ltd.
A subsidiary of Scholastic Inc., New York, 10012 (USA).
Publishers since 1920, with international operations in Canada,
Australia, New Zealand, the United Kingdom, India, and
Hong Kong.

For information regarding permission, write to:
Scholastic India Pvt. Ltd.
A-27, Ground Floor, Sigma Centre
Infocity-1, Sector 34, Gurgaon-122001 (India)

First edition: January 2025

ISBN-13: 978-93-5954-194-5

Printed in India at Shree Maitrey Printech Pvt. Ltd., Noida

A MAGICAL YAOSANG

Linthoi Ningthoujam

A NOTE BY THE AUTHOR

When I thought of writing fiction for young readers, I was instantly reminded of my childhood memories of Yaosang. It was that time of the year we looked forward to the most: a time not just of fun and enjoyment, but also of friendships which continue till this very day. Back then, we did not know much of Yaosang's religious and cultural significance. People all across the world have been celebrating the arrival of spring. Yaosang is a celebration in the same spirit. During this festival, which starts on the full moon day of Lamta (February-March), the Meitei community of Manipur commemorates the onset of spring. The majority of the Meiteis practise a blend of native Meitei and Hindu cultures and customs. This is reflected in the rites and rituals of Yaosang, making it special in its own way.

A unique feature of Yaosang is its association with sporting festivals. The small state of Manipur has produced several sportspersons over the years. At the time of writing this note, Ashalata Devi, a Manipuri, became the first centurion of Indian women's football team. However, I would like to uphold the sporting spirit—the bond over playing together, the diverse strengths each of us has, the grace we show when we fall short, the laughter with which we get over a tumble, and the memories of a lifetime—rather than the competition.

Against this backdrop of Yaosang, this story attempts to introduce young readers to an everyday life in Imphal, the capital of Manipur. I hope this will encourage them to know more about this beautiful state of India.

Lastly, I wish young readers to dream and live the magic of life.

COIN

Red
Yellow
Orange
Red yellow orange
Redyelloworange
Grey
Grey?
Why is this grey interrupting the redyelloworange?

Ten-year-old Bembem was lost in the colours of the evening sky when grey smoke curled up towards the horizon. It was the first day of the spring festival, Yaosang, and the full moon peeped out from the eastern hills. Bembem, her best friend, Meme, and Meme's brother, Tonton, had been waiting for the burning of the Yaosang hut, which would officially mark the beginning of the festival.

Eagerness of young and old alike could be seen in the crowd surrounding the makeshift straw hut at the leikai's ground. Most girls wore red or yellow phanek and matching phee, with small bags hanging on their shoulders. Boys wore shorts and shirts in colours of spring—green, orange, and red. These children dotted not only the leikai's ground, but every gate and every corner of the leikai. The scene was repeated in almost all leikai, and the whole of Imphal wore a festive look.

After the priest had finished the rituals and prayers, the hut was burnt down with cheers from the crowd. Grey smoke from the hut filled the air, and the children knew they could finally go for nakatheng and collect money from house to house.

Bembem, Meme, and Tonton were greeted by the sweet fragrance of jasmine at the gate of their first house.

On other days, they would have discussed a thousand things before entering someone's house—from the size of dogs to probable ghosts on frangipani trees. But it was Yaosang and they had every right to enter any house they wished to! So, through the half-opened gate, head held high, they walked in.

A middle-aged woman was sitting on a reed mat near the main entrance of the house. Next to her, hibiscus flowers were neatly arranged on a brass plate. On another plate, a few sweets were placed.

'We are here for nakatheng. Please give us money,' said the three of them in unison and went up to the veranda.

'Please take these sweets. And bless my home,' said the woman, giving them a rupee each with a beaming smile.

'May you stay happy and prosper,' replied the children.

One after the other, they covered the houses of their leikai. They were, however, not very happy with the amount collected. Standing by the side of the river, they were strategizing how to increase their nakatheng, when Bembem saw the reflection of the moon wavering on the surface of the water.

Something suddenly struck her, and she proposed, 'Let us go to the other side of the river.'

'But we never go to the other side of the river,' said Meme. 'It's too far. We are not supposed to go that far.'

'We can go to the other side and roam about for a while. It is too early in the evening for our parents to start searching for us.'

As the orange moon steadily climbed up the slowly darkening sky, they crossed the small bridge and reached the other side of the river.

They couldn't decide which house to enter first. Bembem asked Tonton to close his eyes and point his finger in any direction he wanted. This was a game they played when they had too many choices and couldn't agree on one.

'Turn me around now,' said Tonton excitedly and closed his eyes.

Meme turned him around and after much deliberation (which the girls felt was unnecessary), Tonton finally pointed his finger.

The girls looked in the direction of his finger and saw an eerie-looking house.

'No, we are not going in there at all,' said Meme.

'It is my choice. Rule is rule. We are going in,' replied Tonton opening his eyes.

'There could be a ghost inside,' Bembem made her point.

'I don't see a frangipani tree, though,' replied Meme.

Finally, curiosity got the better of them, and the group went towards the house. Slowly opening the gate, they stood at the courtyard and started arguing who should go in first.

Suddenly, the courtyard lit up and an old woman came

out. While the three of them froze, the old woman said in a sweet voice, 'Ah, it's you children! I was wondering who must be here to meet me.'

The woman looked at them and deduced they must be there for nakatheng. Asking them to wait, she went inside her house.

When she came out, she pointed at Bembem.

'You look like someone I know,' she said. 'Here, come, take this coin.'

Thanking and blessing the woman, Bembem took the coin. In the faint light of the courtyard, she looked at the coin and saw something about it was different.

The three decided they should not roam anymore but return to collect nakatheng from the remaining houses of their

leikai. To their joy, all the houses gave them ₹5 each. Not a rupee less. They had collected much more than they imagined.

Bembem reached home and tallied the total amount of the day's nakatheng. ₹153! It was her best nakatheng ever.

Preparing to sleep, she listed down activities for the next four days of Yaosang—eating singju, throwing water balloons, participating in sporting events, and dancing at the Thabal Chongba. She then remembered the unusual coin. Getting up in a jiffy, she opened her bag and took out the coin. It had a football etched on one side.

Tha tha
Thabungton
Nacha morambee
Pobige
Tha tha
Thabungton

(O Moon
O glowing Moon
Let me carry your dear child
on my back
O Moon
O glowing Moon)

Ima, her mother, was singing the moon lullaby, carrying Bembem on her back with a naahong. She walked gently from their courtyard towards the gate where their pomelo tree grew.

'Ima, look, the pomelo fruits are becoming bigger!' Bembem exclaimed.

'Oh my! Those are not pomelos! The tree is bearing many moons!' replied Ima, looking at the tree.

'Look at the sky above, Ima. There is a pomelo there instead of the moon.'

'Yes, how strange! I think we should pluck all the moons and take down the pomelo. We can put them in their right places.' Saying this, Ima untied the naahong and put down Bembem.

Then Ima grew taller and taller. Her hands reached for the sky, and she took down the moon.

Next, she shook the tree. All the moons rolled down and gathered near Bembem's feet.

Ima collected the pomelo and the moons in her hands and cupped them.

'Bem, look, they all fit in my hands,' she said, bringing her hands closer to Bembem's face.

Slowly, she opened her hands and there was the coin, and nothing else.

SILVERBERRIES

The next morning, Bembem woke up with a start. What a strange dream it was! Remembering the coin, Bembem looked for her bag and opened it. To her surprise, she found a ₹100 note and a ₹50 note, and not a single coin.

Her father had just come in to wake her up. On seeing her with her bag and looking confused, he explained that he had taken her coins when she was asleep and replaced them with notes. A few children had come to their house early in the morning, and he needed change to give them their nakatheng.

Bembem was convinced that Baba had given away her lucky coin.

Coin, my coin. And that dream!

She couldn't help thinking of it.

Ever since Ima had been hospitalized, Bembem never saw her in her dreams, no matter how much she missed and thought of her. But last night's dream was different. She tried to give herself some sort of explanation. Everything came down to the coin—the eerie house, the woman who seemed to recognize her, the coin, and the nakatheng after the coin. She was surer than ever that it indeed was her lucky coin.

Bembem was still sulking when Meme came over with Tonton. She recounted to them how Baba gave away the coin. 'DO YOU WANT YOUR COIN BACK?' Meme asked in a baritone voice to lift her friend's mood.

'Yes,' Bembem squeaked.

'Let us go on an adventure then. You, me, and Tonton, on a Yaosang adventure!'

After much enquiry, the girls came to realize that Baba had given a few coins to a leikai boy. The task then was to search for this boy, *a* boy, among *all* the boys of their leikai! But before beginning the search, they decided to have breakfast first and went to the food stall. They found children gathered in groups around the food stall.

It seemed all the children of the leikai had come out in the streets, ready for the celebration. Some had already started throwing water balloons at one another. The neighbourhood was full of a vibrant energy. The laughter of children and youngsters could be heard everywhere. Such was the spirit of Yaosang!

'...pomelo tree which bears fruit all season…'

Bembem turned to see who the speaker was. It was a boy who went to the same school with her. He was talking to his friends about his nakatheng visits that morning. The pomelo tree in Bembem's house was famous because it bore fruit all seasons long. Since the boy mentioned it, he, of course, had been to Bembem's house.

Bembem went to the boy and asked, 'Did my father give you any coins?'

'No,' said the boy. 'Why do you ask?'

There was an unsaid rule that no one had the right to ask about the whys and wherefores of a child's nakatheng. He was convinced that Bembem was in a serious trouble; otherwise, she would not break the rule.

'What happened? Is everything alright?' He was determined to help.

'It's nothing. I think my father gave away my lucky coin.'

'Lucky coin? That's a trouble!' he sympathetically said. 'Maybe you can get it back. Do you know Lukhoi, the one with curly hair, whose house is always guarded by a big black dog with huge fangs? I think I saw your father giving him coins.'

Bembem had never spoken to Lukhoi nor knew where he lived. But she knew Bungbung, Lukhoi's friend. So, she asked Meme and Tonton to come with her to Bungbung's house, forgetting all about her breakfast.

The trio stood at Bungbung's courtyard and waited for someone to come out of the house.

Bembem looked at the ripe silverberry fruits dropping down on the homestead's shrine. She used to come here often with Ima who was friends with Bungbung's mother. They exchanged nursery plants and discussed fruits, vegetables, and the most suitable season for their plantation.

Bungbung's mother also visited Ima's vast garden in the afternoon. They would walk and talk, talk and walk—from the courtyard to the rows of cabbage—till late evening. However, for the past few months, it looked desolate and many plants didn't flower.

Bembem was still admiring the silverberries when Bungbung's father came out.

'Sorry, Bembem. Bungbung has gone to the toy store with Lukhoi.'

None of the three had ever been on a rickshaw without an adult. There was a sense of worry but also a newfound boldness at their own independence. As it was Bembem's coin, she took the initiative. Gathering courage, she approached a rickshaw. 'To…to the main market, please…'

On the way, they saw young boys and girls chasing and throwing water balloons at one another. Some hid behind balconies and gates and used water guns to aim.

The rickshaw crossed the leikai's ground, decorated with flags of different colours in preparation for the annual Yaosang sports meet. Elderly volunteers were busy cleaning the ground for the inauguration ceremony. For a while, the sight of the colourful festivities made Bembem forgot why they were going to the market.

The toy shop was managed by a girl their age. The three went up to her.

'Hello, could you do us a favour, please?' Bembem requested. 'We believe a boy bought toys from your store with my lucky coin. Could you please look into your cash box and check for any unusual coin? You see, it is my lucky coin. I must get it back.'

An adult would have thought of this as a trivial matter, but since both parties were children, they knew the importance of lucky objects in their lives.

The girl asked no further questions, but simply said, 'My father forbids me from opening the cash box unless it is to put in money from a sale. Would you like to buy anything?'

Bembem turned back to the group, and they huddled to discuss matters. To save money for their fare back home, they decided to buy only two water balloons.

Opening the cash box, the girl put in the money from the sale and took out a few coins for them to see.

Bembem squinted her eyes, taking a long look. Dismay set over her face. Her lucky coin was not there.

Meanwhile, the girl's father came out. When they narrated their problem, he identified two boys who gave him a ₹20 note, but no coin.

Bembem's disappointment changed to relief. She figured their next step was to begin their return journey and find Bungbung and Lukhoi.

It was almost noon, and the day was getting hot. As luck would have it, they found the same rickshaw parked near the shop and jumped on it.

On the way back, Tonton started throwing the balloons at a boy standing by the side of the road. The boy returned with another balloon. Water splashed and the rickshaw was filled with excitement.

Phreeeeeee

What was that sound?

Phreeeeeee

'Please move aside!' blared the loudspeaker. 'Let our athletes run.'

The rickshaw pulled to the side, and all of them turned to look.

Lily Kamei was bearing the ceremonial torch from Kangla. She was leading the contingent and running in front of young people and children. All the runners except for Lily Kamei wore white T-shirts printed with the logo of their leikai's club. Lily Kamei wore the captain jersey of the national football team. Under her captaincy, the team had enjoyed much success in international competitions the previous year.

The torch run, akin to the torch relay of the Olympics, would formally flag off the sports meet. Every leikai organizing Yaosang sports meet would take the opportunity of this ceremonial run to pay respect to lead sportspersons.

'Please move aside for Ms Lily Kamei.' The loudspeaker continued. 'Let us thank her for her contribution to the country and to the future of sports in the state. We also thank her for agreeing to grace our leikai's sports meet.'

Bembem could not stop staring at Ms Lily's arms. They clearly exhibited signs of muscular strength as she held the flaming torch against the bright light of the sun. Bembem was awestruck with Ms Lily's running form. She had once visited Bembem's football training session and showed some of her tactics. For the many young people of the leikai, including Bembem, Lily Kamei was an inspiration.

With her mother in the hospital and Baba constantly running around and managing household chores and their electronics store, Bembem had been missing many football sessions. But watching Ms Lily run made Bembem stand with a renewed vigour to run like her one day. For her, the best part of football was not goal-scoring, but running—running with the wind, running with friends, running with the ball.

Seeing children following the runners to the ground, Bembem had a feeling they would surely find Bungbung and Lukhoi at the ground too.

The ground was alive with activities: club volunteers preparing for the forthcoming events; loudspeaker playing the latest songs; children looking forward to the events; some dancing to the songs.

Bembem looked far and wide. At last, at the southern end of the ground, under the shade of the heavily blossoming mango tree, she saw a figure.

Bungbung lay on the grass with his eyes closed. His hands were up in the air tracing a shape.

'What are you doing?' asked Bembem.

'Who is disturbing me?' Bungbung was startled and opened his eyes swiftly. 'I was drawing such a wonderful elephant in the clouds. Now, its shape is gone!'

'Drawing? With your eyes closed?'

'We artists have an inward vision. Children will not understand.'

'Never mind. Where is Lukhoi?'

'He's not with me, as you can see. Why ask?'

'Tell us where he is. He came to my house in the morning, and I think Baba gave him my lucky coin by mistake.'

'Then go and find him. Why are you bothering me?'

'We don't know his house. Could you come with us, please?'

'I cannot go to Lukhoi's house. His father came to find him and saw us standing here instead of joining the torch run. That disappointed him a bit. You see, we are art lovers, and observing nature is our daily activity. His father thinks otherwise.'

Meme and Tonton were bored and confused with Bungbung's way of talking, but Bembem knew that was his way: more adultlike.

'Could you help us find him in the evening? Please?' requested Bembem.

As aloof as Bungbung sounded, Bembem knew his kind heart and appealed to it. Finally, he agreed to help her.

Extreme hunger kicked in as they walked back home. Bembem smelled a whiff of roasted ngaari. She suddenly remembered the kaangsoi her mother used to make. Peas, potatoes, and tomatoes, with onion leaves and ginger, boiled in a broth of fermented fish called ngaari and smoked fish. Pour it on hot rice, and you'd have the healthiest, most wholesome meal.

Bembem used to have kaangsoi every day after school before her mother dropped her off to her football session. She longed for her mother's cooking. No matter how much her father tried, his kaangsoi just didn't have the right taste.

Sometimes Bembem felt bad for Baba. He did whatever a parent could to make her comfortable. But she just missed her mother even though she didn't show it.

Bembem was about to enter the gate to her house when Meme pulled her aside.

'Look, we will find your coin,' said Meme. 'Don't think about it too much. By the way, my mother has invited you for dinner tomorrow. Don't forget.'

Bembem smiled and thanked her best friend. What would she do without her! Her friend, her companion!

Meme understood that, apart from the coin, Bembem was bothered about her mother being in the hospital. She didn't know how to talk about it or whether she should talk about it at all. Bembem herself hardly mentioned her mother. But Meme would always come up with ways to cheer up her friend.

Bembem's lunch was laid on a platter and covered properly. Baba must have missed her during lunch and, hence, the platter.

'Are you back? We waited for you for so long. You should not wander off without telling us,' said a concerned Baba from the backyard.

In the last few months, her father had become less strict. According to him, it was because Bembem was a big girl and should learn to be responsible for herself. It was true that she had her circle of friends. Most of the time, they lived in a world of their own. But sometimes, she wanted to be the naughty, pampered girl who was teased by close ones, play with her Ima, and run to hide behind the gooseberry tree.

She didn't want to be a big girl. Not yet.

Bembem sat down and began to eat. Unless it was her mother's kaangsoi, she didn't feel like eating. However, there was a sense of guilt for missing the family meal, and she decided to eat Baba's kaangsoi without any fuss. She poured the broth over the glutinous rice, took a big handful, and ate.

Oh my god, what taste! It is exactly like Ima's!

For a moment, she felt her mother was back; her mother was home.

After lunch, Bembem rested for a while. Closing her eyes, she thought of the evening's plan to find her coin. She then got up to take a bath at the bathing area next to their pond.

There was an overcast cloud. Bembem loved the rain and calling for it, slowly hummed:

Nong O churo
Hanuba hanubi taotharo
Langjing maton thumhatlo

Nong O churo
(Let there be rain
Let the old be washed away
Let it flood the Langjing peak
Let there be rain)

She immediately realized the rain might spoil her evening. 'I should sing about sunshine instead.'

Nungsa o saaro
Urum Leima changkharo
(Let there be sunshine
Let the dark clouds drift away)

'Now, there will be no rain,' she murmured to herself and went to fetch water from the pond.

Plop plop plop.

What was that?

She looked down at the water to see what the sound was.

Plop, plop.

She looked up.

What! When did this happen!

Their silverberry plant was heavy with over-ripened fruits. A bunch of the juicy red fruits speckled with silver dust hung on the branch overlooking the pond. Baba had been lamenting that their plant had not blossomed that year. Ima's garden had come to a standstill, or at least slowed down after she became ill. But on seeing the fruits, Bembem was amazed.

When did it flower? When did it bear fruits?

How did no one notice?

She quickly took a bath and got ready to meet Meme.

On the way out, she saw her grandmother washing brass items for the evening prayer.

'Bobok!' Bembem called out. 'Our silverberry is bearing fruits! I have plucked a few ripe ones for your evening prayer.'

It had been a long time since Bobok saw her granddaughter talking in her chirpy voice. She looked keenly at the child,

untimely turning into a young adult in the absence of the mother. Her eyes were soon clouded with tears.

O, mother of Bembem, when will you return and hold this child to your bosom again?

The ground was hustling and bustling with people—audience, participants, potential participants, and random children running around.

Bembem, Meme, Tonton, and Bungbung saw a heavy crowd gathered at the eastern side of the ground. The probability of Lukhoi being part of the crowd was high, and they went there to look for him.

'Now, we have a mukna competition between Longjam Dhojo and Sinam Loken for the senior men's championship,' the loudspeaker announced.

Longjam Dhojo was Bungbung's father. Bungbung, of course, wanted to see his father play. So, the group decided to watch and cheer for Bungbung's father, and search for Lukhoi after the match. Moreover, it was the first time their club included mukna, the Meitei's traditional form of wrestling, at the Yaosang festival.

Mukna was an ancient sport, and the young audience did not know how points were scored. All they knew was that the opponents had to tackle each other, obtain an advantageous position, and pin the other with their back touching the ground.

Unknown to Bembem's generation, Longjam Dhojo and Sinam Loken were skilled players—their fitness and endurance were equally matched. As the game proceeded, none of them could score the winning move.

The audience grew excited. Their chants were divided between 'Dhojo' and 'Loken'.

Someone shouted 'Loishallo, get it over with!', to which Dhojo turned to the side and looked at the spectator scornfully. Taking advantage of the moment, Loken pushed a little. Dhojo lost his balance, and Loken easily pinned him to the ground.

The audience roared with excitement at the turn of events and laughter at Dhojo's slip of balance.

The opponents maintained grace, hugged, congratulated each other, and bowed to the crowd. Bungbung's face gleamed with pride.

Slowly, the crowd dispersed.

Bembem saw young boys and girls lining up in two long queues. She lost sight of Bungbung and went near the queues to search for him. All the children were taller than her. She could not make out whether Bungbung or Lukhoi were part of the queues. Craning her neck and tiptoeing, she looked around for them.

'We are now ready for the tug of war for the mixed-team, sub-junior category,' said the voice on the loudspeaker.

There was a loud cheer from the queues. A volunteer pushed Bembem a little, and she found herself at the front of the line-up. She was about to leave the spot, when suddenly she saw Lukhoi ready to take the rope for the opponent team.

This is my chance! Bembem thought if she participated, she would not lose sight of Lukhoi and her coin would be found.

'Participants are requested to warm-up. At the sound of the whistle, please begin the game,' the loudspeaker again blared.

As much as Bembem would have wanted to go up to Lukhoi and talk, she knew the importance of a good warm-up before a game and did some stretches. Taking her position, she waited for the sound of the whistle.

Phreeeeeee

'Chingo, chingo. Pull pull.'

All were shouting from different directions.

The rope moved in the opponent's direction. Everyone was straining out their energy. Bembem also gave her best and tugged on the rope. She could feel the rope moving back as they pulled together, and then the rope came back to the neutral position.

The pulling resumed with full might from both teams.

The crowd kept cheering, 'Yaa…yaaaa, pull, pull.'

Lukhoi was playing for the opponent team and was second in line from the centre. Bembem saw him clenching his teeth, squinting his eyes, and pulling with all the force he had. Bembem also closed her eyes and pulled…*yaaaaaaa*…

In a sudden burst, appeared a vision: Lukhoi's face turned into the coin! Bembem opened her eyes, and all members of the other team had the face of the coin!

Instead of being stunned, she shouted, '*Yaaaaaa*… Give me back MY COIN!' and pulled the rope towards herself with all her might.

Bembem's team had won the match.

From the corner of her eye, Bembem could see Ms Lily running towards her. She looked excited. 'How do you have so much strength and endurance in that little body? I have seen you play football. You are indeed an athlete.'

At these words from Ms Lily, Bembem forgot her mission behind coming to the ground. Ms Lily shook her hands and Bembem smiled back in gratitude. When she turned around, Lukhoi was gone.

On their way back home, Bembem, Meme, and Tonton didn't talk about the coin at all. They seemed to have forgotten the purpose of the day's adventure. Their focus was on the splendid day they'd had.

After dinner, Bembem was in bed when Baba came in. 'Everyone was only talking about you after that tug of war game!'

How embarrassing! For a moment, Bembem thought it was because they might have heard her scream about taking back the coin.

'It seemed you helped your team win the game,' said Baba proudly. 'I thought you had lost all your stamina

after missing so many football sessions. Won't you start playing again?'

Bembem wanted to say yes, but all she could manage was, 'I don't know, Baba.'

Baba knew how much his daughter had changed after his wife's illness. They had first begun to take Bembem for football sessions because of her active temperament. His friends had suggested Bembem try sports like boxing which was rather popular in Manipur, or gymnastics which was gaining popularity. But Ima had refused.

'Bembem might feel suffocated in a ring or an indoor stadium,' Ima had said to him. 'Let her run around freely and have fun too. She should not focus much on training or winning. Let her enjoy a good game with the leikai's children at our nearby ground. I think she might like football.'

Like? Bembem loved it.

Red silverberries dropped from the tree and landed on the moon's reflection on the pond. A hand with a single gold bangle on wrist picked up the fruits slowly.

'Bem, let's pluck them directly from the plant. Shall we?' It was Ima's voice. She slowly dropped stones...one, two, three, four...on the moon's reflection, sending ripples throughout the pond.

When the stones finally stacked up, Ima jumped on top of them. She stretched out her arm and helped Bembem up too. On her tiptoes, she tried to reach the fruits, their silver speckles shining in the moonlight. The stacked stones suddenly grew higher and higher and started moving.

'Ima, be careful!' shouted Bembem, holding on Ima's phanek. Ima grabbed the branch overhead, but the stones gave away and she started falling…

Falling…

Falling…

Thud!

Ima and Bembem landed on a firm surface and water splashed all around.

'Wow! No broken bones, Bem!'

Bembem turned to her side and saw they had landed on a round surface. First, she thought it was a metallic lotus leaf. But the surface was rough to touch. She moved her

hands around to feel what it could be. Hexagons, pentagons, hexagons, pentagons… It was the design of a football.

They had landed on her lucky coin!

Just then, all the red silverberries started falling on them softly. Amazed at this magnificent sight, Ima laughed and hugged Bembem warmly.

Bembem woke up from yet another strange dream. To say that these dreams were not bothering her would be an understatement. She was sweating profusely and wondered if she was going to be sick. Nevertheless, she got up. Sick or not, she had to find her coin somehow.

U-MOROK

As Bembem and Meme slowly opened the gate to Lukhoi's house, they almost collided with Lukhoi himself.

'Aren't you the kids from fourth standard?' asked Lukhoi.

'Yes, we are. I am Bembem. I wanted to ask if…'

'Yes, I know. Bungbung told me you had been searching for your coin.'

'Do you have it?'

'Have what?'

'The coin?'

'No, not at all!'

Bembem looked at Lukhoi in disbelief.

'You seem to be in shock. It's just a coin,' said Lukhoi.

'It's a coin with…'

'I don't want to know.' Lukhoi cut her short.

Why do all sixth standard students talk like this? Meme stared at him.

'My grandmother had to go to the big temple and wanted coins to offer there. She took them all from me yesterday afternoon. You see, there was no coin with me when you came searching yesterday.' Lukhoi looked amused.

'Could you ask your grandmother if we could see her coins?' Bembem pleaded.

'Yes, I could, but she is already at the temple. You better hurry before she offers them all.'

Mostly, elderly people in white and pinkish-white traditional attire gathered at the gate of the big temple. Their clothes were identical: white pheijom and pumyaat for the men, pinkish-white phanek, and white phee for the women. Bobok wore a similar attire, with a white ginger lily flower adorning her hair. She was part of their leikai's nupi pala, a group of women performers who sang devotional songs. That day, they had come to offer their prayers. Bembem knew that Bobok was going there and requested her to take them along. She was also friends with Lukhoi's grandmother.

Telling the children to stay inside the temple complex, Bobok climbed up the steps to the temple hall. Her face suddenly had the calmness of the dawn sky as she joined the sea of devotees.

'How are we ever going to find Lukhoi's grandmother in this crowd?' Bembem asked disappointedly. 'I can't even see where my own Bobok went!'

Meme looked at Bembem. They were best friends and did everything together—from attending the same class, wearing matching sandals, eating salty sundried wild apple on balmy winter days, and collecting flowers for pressing. All, except playing football. Meme never understood Bembem's craze for football. Or, for that matter, how a single coin held such power over her. Meme had once heard her aunt talk of a cousin possessed by spirits. Her aunt had to take the help of one maibi to ward off the spirit.

However, Meme concluded it couldn't be a spirit. Unlike her cousin, Bembem was not walking alone at night, speaking in foreign tongues, nor breaking into random bouts of dancing or laughing. Meme had been concerned ever since Bembem's mother was taken to the hospital. But Meme knew something else was going on ever since the coin had appeared, and she needed to look out for her friend.

A canopy of bottlebrushes hung over the temple's pond. By the waterbody, a smaller temple stood in all its serenity. Bembem, Meme, and Tonton decided to take a tour of the area. They could hear the rhythm of the traditional musical instrument, pung, accompanied by mandira and singing from the hall.

When they reached the small temple, each decided to ring the temple bells, each one louder than the last.

Kang

Kang kang

Kangkangkangkangkangkangkangkangkaaaaaaaaaang…

The three of them started giggling.

Out of nowhere, Tonton came up with the most outrageous idea. 'Let's sort out all the coins on the offering plate and see if the lucky coin is there!'

'Are you crazy, Ton?' Meme scoffed. 'If we are caught, everyone will think we were trying to steal.'

'There are so many coins here,' said Bembem, thinking it wasn't a bad idea. 'My lucky coin could be among them. Chances are high. Tonton can be on the lookout while we check. Come on, don't be a spoilsport, Meme!'

Meme was reluctant. She had a feeling that their adventure might go out of hand. Nevertheless, she agreed.

Coins jingled and jangled while they looked.

'By the way, how would I know which one is the lucky coin?' asked Meme.

'It is the size of a one-rupee coin but one side has…' Bembem was interrupted by Tonton's whistling, signalling someone's approach.

Bembem and Meme sat still.

'What are you children doing here?' a tall, elderly man stooped down and asked them.

'We are sorry. We didn't mean to…' Bembem started apologizing.

'It's okay. You can ring the bells, but don't play with them. Now, where are your parents?'

It was enough escapade for the day, and the three returned to the temple hall and sat down on its cool steps.

Bembem looked around. People were praying intently, their heads bowed in reverence and eyes closed in meditation.

What are they praying for?

Boy in green shorts, do you want to pluck clouds and put them in your pocket?

Woman on the right, do you want to string stars and weave them into your phanek?

Man on the left, do you want to build a house up in the sky?

What will I pray for? Ima to come back?

Does God really give what one asks for?

'Bembem! Bembem!' It was Meme. 'I think you need to see a maibi. You are so lost these days. Bobok is calling.'

The children went over to where Bobok was sitting and requested her to take them to Lukhoi's grandmother.

Lukhoi's grandmother was chatting with a few devotees at the side of the hall.

'There you are. These children are asking for you. God knows why,' said a confused Bobok to Lukhoi's grandmother.

'What is it, children?' asked Lukhoi's grandmother.

'Lukhoi's grandma,' said Bembem, 'did you take some coins from Lukhoi yesterday? One of my coins was mistakenly taken. We wanted to ask you about it.'

Lukhoi's grandmother looked puzzled.

'Did Lukhoi send you?' she asked. 'That boy is very particular when it comes to his things. I don't know anything about your coin. However, I did give some coins to his sister in the morning. You can ask her. Let's go home now, it's getting late.'

It was just after noon when they reached Bembem's house. Meme decided it was time she and Tonton return home too.

'Wait, Meme!' said Bembem, taking Meme's hand. 'Let's go to Lukhoi's house and look for his sister,'

'Bembem, I am so tired. My mother told me to return early today. We have lots of chores at home.'

'But, Meme, we might lose the coin forever!'

'Bembem, please don't be angry. We have done everything we could to look for your coin. But you don't even bother to tell us why it is so important. It's Yaosang, and I want to enjoy the festival. We haven't even played with water or colour this time. I want to play Yaosang, don't you?

'I do.'

'By the way, there is the dinner tonight at my house. You must have forgotten about it in the quest for your coin,' said Meme exasperatedly before leaving.

Bembem asked her father to buy some colour powder before going to Meme's house. She knew Meme was right, and she had to make up to her.

Meme lived with her mother and Tonton. Her uncles lived next to their house, and her cousins visited often. That evening, Meme's mother had invited all the seven cousins.

Bembem and Meme enjoyed the company of the cousins, especially the older girls. Their stories and anecdotes would keep them entertained for hours. They sometimes pampered the two with colourful hair clips and spicy singju.

Bembem's mood was instantly lifted when she saw one of the cousins, plucking coriander from the small garden.

Bembem stepped in quietly. She poured some colour powder on her hand, smeared the cousin's face from behind, and giggled like a small child.

When the cousin saw it was Bembem, she too laughed. She then took the small bucket kept for washing coriander and splashed its water on Bembem.

One by one, the other cousins, Meme, and Tonton all came out to the garden. When they saw Yaosang being played at the courtyard, some ran into their houses, brought out their water guns and colour powder, and started playing to the fullest.

The elders came out to see the commotion and kept shouting 'Get over with it'; 'You will feel cold'; and 'Oh, these children'. But none of them took their elders seriously. In the end, the elders gave up, brought out their stools, and watched, smiling at the youngsters.

Bembem was laughing all the while when suddenly, she was standing face-to-face with Meme. They couldn't stay mad at each other for long. Both of them smiled and smeared coloured powder on each other's faces and reconciled.

'Meme, I am sorry,' said Bembem. 'I will not talk about the coin now. Let's enjoy Yaosang. Tomorrow is the last day of the sports meet. We can go to the ground and watch some events.'

'Bembem, why is the coin so important to you? I know that our nakatheng was a success after we got the coin. But something tells me there is more to it.'

'Are you sure you won't take me to the maibi if I tell you?'

'Are you possessed? Did you pluck any wild flower? My aunt says we should never pluck any wild flower!'

'I don't know. I am having these strange dreams. I keep seeing the coin along with my mother. I never saw Ima in my dreams before I got that coin. Do you think I need to go to the maibi?'

'It is strange, but as long as you are not behaving like my fourth cousin, I think you are fine.' Meme thought it was better not to scare Bembem or spoil the evening. 'Those dreams must be impossible dreams, maku-mang.'

Bembem felt better and thought her dreams indeed were impossible dreams. She hoped they wouldn't happen again.

The fourth cousin came in to call them out for dinner.

Bembem looked at him. *He looks like any other boy. How is he possessed?*

'Dada, is it true you were possessed and your mother took you to a maibi?'

'What a joke!' said the fourth cousin with a laugh. 'Are you spreading rumours? Do I look possessed? I sleepwalk. My scared mother took me to a maibi. Yet the maibi couldn't help. You know why? Because I. Am. Not. POSSESSED.'

Bembem was relieved that strange things could happen without being possessed by spirits.

The aroma of soiboom eromba filled the air of the makeshift kitchen in the courtyard. The older cousins were helping Meme's mother prepare the eromba, the ingredients of which had been pre-boiled. One was peeling the small red potatoes; another was sorting out the inch-cut taro stems and the fermented bamboo shoots, soiboom. The eldest was mashing red chillies with ngaari into a thick paste. The paste would then be mixed with the rest of the ingredients.

It was the third day after full moon. The night-blooming jasmine was dispersing its sweet fragrance. The cousins had specifically requested Meme's mother to arrange their small party in the courtyard, under the clear night sky.

Bembem did not have cousins on her father's side, and she hadn't visited her maternal cousins in a long time. She loved the banter among Meme's cousins. It reminded her of the occasional visits to Ima's natal home when Ima was in the prime of her health. She saw her mother's demeanour changed to that of a little child's whenever they were there. Bembem cherished that side of her mother—laughing freely, her hair open, swimming in the river holding a brass pitcher, and plucking berries. Bembem had often thought if Ima had been a child of her age, they would definitely be best friends and could play football together. The thought made a smile appear on her face. *Ima and football? No way! Ima hardly knows how to kick a ball!*

Chicken stewed slowly on firewood. Meme's mother garnished it with culantro, giving the main dish its finishing touch. Apart from the stew and soiboom eromba, there were boiled chayote chunks, and a special accompanying dish—u-morok metpa. It was a paste made of ngaari and u-morok, mashed together and garnished with finely chopped herbs like fish-mint and coriander.

One by one, banana leaves were laid out. Dinner was served, beginning with piping hot rice. After the excitement of playing with water guns and colour powder and the fits of laughter that followed, Bembem was famished and ready to lick her leaf clean.

'Bembem, do you want this u-morok metpa? Have you ever tasted u-morok?' asked the eldest cousin before serving.

'No, Che, I have never tried it, but would like to.' Bembem had read in a magazine that u-morok was known by different names in different parts of Northeast India where it grows. The magazine also mentioned that it was declared the world's hottest chilli in the Guinness World Records in 2007.

The aroma of the world's hottest chilli gave her the jitters. But seeing all the cousins and even Meme relish it, Bembem felt left out and decided to give it a try. She believed tasting it was a rite of passage, which Meme had already crossed.

It is my turn today. Bembem thought.

'Just take a little on your fingertip and try it first.' Meme's mother suggested.

Bembem carefully tasted it. *Okay, this is unusual, but tasty. I think I like u-morok.*

The red bits of u-morok among the white fish-mint root and green coriander caught her eyes and Bembem decided to try it again. This time, the red bit.

Ho Ima! What is happening to me?! Why am I suddenly seeing lights?

Am I dying? I am dying.

I can't see anything now!

I AM DEAD!

'Is she dead?'

'Don't be silly.'

'Relax, she will come around.'

'What will I say to her father? I am so embarrassed.'

'I have heard of fainting spells after consuming u-morok.'

'What time is it now?' asked Bembem, opening her eyes.

'Are you okay? Does your stomach hurt?' said Meme's mother.

'No, I am fine but what happened? I thought I was dying,' said Bembem.

'You ate too much u-morok,' the eldest cousin remarked.

'Don't over act now, Bembem. You were out for hardly ten seconds,' another cousin joked.

Bembem looked around and saw there was a power cut.

'It went dark all of sudden and I thought I was dying,' she said with a sigh of relief.

All of them started laughing at the unusual coincidence. Bembem also joined in.

Baba had cleaned Bembem's room, changed sheets, and arranged her study table. Everything looked different. It felt different but Bembem had no energy left to think. As soon as she lay down on her bed, she fell into a deep slumber.

Gham
Gham
Gham

'What are you weaving, Ima?' asked Bembem.

The sky had a hint of pink, marking the arrival of the sun. Apart from the chirping of a few early birds and the sound of Ima weaving on her backstrap loom, there was silence all around.

'Oh, this? This is your phanek for the coming Yaosang. Don't you think it's lovely?' said Ima, hands separating the yellow threads, her eyes focused on weaving.

'It is lovely. But what are these red designs on the border?' Bembem came up to her to take a closer look.

'Oh, these are u-morok motifs.'

'But isn't it unusual to weave this motif on a phanek?'

'It is. But I plucked all these red u-moroks yesterday, and I was inspired.' Ima showed Bembem her basket where the spools were kept. But there was no spool in it, only u-morok. Ima took up one u-morok and weaved it in the phanek.

Those are not motifs! Those are real u-morok!

How can one ever wear clothes with u-morok on them, let alone its motif!

'Don't worry, dear. If you don't like this design, I can put another motif on it.' It was as if Ima had heard Bembem's thought.

'Well, to be honest, I don't like it at all.'

'Alright, then. I will use this motif. Open my hand and see for yourself,' said Ima, putting out her right hand, tightly clenched into a fist.

Bembem looked at Ima's hand and wondered. She bent down to see what it was.

It was the coin.

FOOTBALL

Father was cleaning the garden when Bembem came out to the courtyard. She looked all around. The whole courtyard had been swept clean. The flower pots were neatly arranged at the veranda, though there were hardly any flowers, except for a few marigolds. Everything looked different. *Something felt different.* But Bembem had no time to ponder, not even about last night's dream. She convinced herself that if she found the coin, her dreams would go away.

'Bembem, the legend has arrived!' Meme teased. 'Everyone in the leikai knows your u-morok incident now. People say u-morok can make a person faint. But we witnessed it yesterday. What a dinner it was!'

'Can you stop it now? I am never eating it again,' said Bembem.

'Hey, I was just kidding. By the way, did you have any dreams about the coin last night?'

'In fact, I did. And I also dreamt of u-morok.'

'See, I told you! You are THE u-morok legend! Now, coming to the coin. I am intrigued. We need to find it and take it to a maibi I know.'

'How do you know so many maibis? All these things you say, Meme. They scare me. Let's not get into it. First, let's go back to Lukhoi's house and find his sister.'

Bembem, Meme, and Tonton met Lukhoi on the way. He was going to the ground to participate in the mathematical race. He told the trio that if they wished to meet his sister, they could go to his house. He also cautioned them not to make too much noise. His father had returned from night duty and was still asleep.

'And don't worry about the dog. Just say his name, Amubi, and he won't bark,' Lukhoi added.

The three slowly nudged the gate to Lukhoi's house and went in. Amubi was nowhere to be seen. Standing at the courtyard, the girls discussed whether to go in further or call out to Lukhoi's sister.

Tonton, paying no heed to the discussion, removed his sandals and went in quietly. The front door was open, and he peeped through the curtains. There had been no electricity since the previous night and, with the house being a traditional Meitei yumjao, the interiors were quite dim.

Tonton saw something bright, and he leaned forward to have a better look. Inside a room, a white figure was moving like a wave. It stood up and became taller and taller. It kept moving and then finally separated. Tonton suddenly realized it was not one, but two white figures, and he froze.

The figures spread their wings and continued their movement, ever so gently. Tonton turned around, clamping his mouth shut, not to let out any cry lest it provoked the ghosts. He was so scared that he didn't see the cat resting near the door, and stepped on its tail.

MeeoowwwWWWW. Out came a high-pitched cry.

'Run! Run! There are ghosts! Run! Run!' Face red as a tomato, Tonton shouted and ran out of the house.

The hullaballoo brought a giant of a dog to the front of the house and woke up Lukhoi's father.

The children could have run away, but the dog started barking at them. And when a dog barks, one should not run. That is the rule, isn't it?

'Amubi, it's alright. Hey Amubi, stop it now!' Lukhoi's father pacified the dog.

Amubi stopped barking and the situation became less tense.

'Who are these children, Father?'

A voice was heard from inside and the white figure came out and removed her veil.

It was Lukhoi's sister. She wore a pale pink phanek with a white blouse. A white phee covered her whole upper body, including her head and face. She removed the phee, and the children saw her wear a small conical headgear.

'It's her! She is possessed and there were two of them!' Tonton screamed shakily.

Since there was no wall between the neighbouring houses, Lukhoi's uncles and aunts had also arrived to ask what the commotion was about. Clearly, the children were not in a state to explain. So, Lukhoi's father turned to his daughter Ahanbi and inquired.

Ahanbi had been smiling all the while.

'I was practising my performance for Halangkar,' she said. 'I don't even know these children. They must have thought I was a ghost in this white cloth.'

'No, there were two of them, and both were very tall!' Tonton put forth his argument.

'You silly boy. There are no ghosts. It was me and my image. I was rehearsing in front of the mirror.' Ahanbi then pointed to her headgear. 'See this headgear? It easily adds a few inches to a person's height.'

The onlookers laughed and tried to lighten the children's mood.

'She is going to perform as a Brajamai at the Halangkar tomorrow,' said Ahanbi's uncle. 'All Brajamais have to wear white veils. You must go to see the performance. There will be hundreds of ghosts there!'

Seeing that Tonton was still in a state of shock, Lukhoi's father asked Ahanbi to make sure the children reach home safely.

Ahanbi brought the children to her room, and they waited while she got ready.

'I think I know you,' said Ahanbi, turning to Meme while combing her long, black hair. 'Your cousin and I are good friends. Our group is meeting in a few minutes now. We are going from house to house to request donations for the Thabal Chongba tomorrow.'

Bembem was now reassured that Ahanbi was friendly and not a ghost. It was time she requested Ahanbi for the coin.

'Che, actually, we came to ask you about a…'

'Is it about a coin?' Ahanbi interrupted. 'Grandmother said some children were searching for a coin which she thinks is with me. To be honest, it could be with me or with her. She is forgetful these days. But, look, children. Look around. My room is so messy. I have been busy with organizing the Yaosang feast, volunteering at the sports meet, and tomorrow is the finale, the Thabal Chongba.'

Bembem didn't say anything further.

Ahanbi's room was indeed in a state of chaos. There were a few shimmery blouses at her table waiting to be ironed out. Her books, which were perhaps on the table before it was turned into an ironing board, were kept on the chair. Her make-up items were scattered at the dressing table. Festive mapaan-naiba phanek of different colours were piled up into a heap on her bed.

Bembem was sitting on the bed, looking around, when she accidentally touched one of the phaneks.

'No, girl, don't touch it!' Ahanbi exclaimed suddenly. 'There is a needle pinned somewhere in the folds of that phanek. I was stitching it last night. I am going to wear it tomorrow at the Thabal. Do you now agree how busy I am?'

Bembem knew how important Thabal Chongba was to young men and women. They were going to be the stars of the evening. They considered it quite important that they looked their best.

'Now, if you don't have any important work, come for the donation drive. I can help find your coin when we return. What do you say?' Ahanbi proposed. 'People just love it when children come for donation during Yaosang, don't they?'

On the way out, Ahanbi looked up at the grey clouds thickening on the horizon. She hastily hung a polaang, a kind of bamboo basket, on a bamboo stand in the courtyard. It was believed that if a polaang is kept in this manner, the rain, worried that its water would be drained through the holes of the basket, will feel useless and decide not to rain at all. One could sense that Ahanbi was trying her best to ward off the rain and not let it ruin Thabal Chongba the next day.

Bembem had started to enjoy the company of Ahanbi and her group. They explained everything with care and pampered the children with singju after the donation drive. They also asked the girls' opinion regarding the colour of the dresses they were going to wear for the Thabal. Sometimes, they treated them as children; sometimes, like their peers. Bembem concluded she made a few good sister-friends that day.

When they were returning and were about to reach Bembem's house, the rain suddenly lashed out. Ahanbi's group sheltered the children with their scarves and dropped them at the house. No words were exchanged regarding the coin. All Bembem could think of was how disappointed Ahanbi and her group would be if the rain continued. She was sad for her new friends.

Darkness engulfed the surroundings, and all plans were cancelled for the evening. The power was still out, and Bembem's family managed to have an early dinner with lanterns.

She was lying with Bobok and told her of the day's events when Baba came in and sat down next to them.

'So, what did you do today?' he asked. 'It seems you have found new friends. You are getting older, my baby girl. After a few years, it will be your group's turn to organize the Thabal Chongba.'

Bembem and Baba hardly had a heart-to-heart talk. When Ima was well, he was seldom home. They had a small shop that sold electronics at the main market and he tended to it, while Ima stayed home with Bembem.

'Could you answer me something, Bembem? Your mother has been in the hospital since December. It is March now. You have visited her just once. Don't you want to see her?'

As Baba asked these uncomfortable questions, Bobok held Bembem tightly, as if saying it was alright to not answer.

'I miss Ima,' answered Bembem.

'I know she cannot answer you nor can see or hug you. But she can hear your voice. She must be missing you just as you miss her.'

Baba's voice broke, and he left the room. In the faint light of the lantern, Bembem could not make out whether he was crying.

The rain showed no sign of slowing down.

The ball passed from one foot to another. Players were running towards the ball, shouting to their teammates.

Bembem looked around. The grass was green. There was a hillock on the eastern side. A majestic peepal tree looked at the field as a silent audience. Cows were grazing on one side of the field, and a football match was happening on another side.

Bembem was in the centre, sitting on a bench. She had never seen this football field. She didn't know where she was.

Jham jham jham

Jham jham jham

Rain came pounding on the field. All the players suddenly wore polaangs over their heads.

Bembem could see a girl in a red jersey running towards the goal line. The opposing team was not able to block the ball, and the girl in red kicked it into the goalpost.

Goal! It was a goal!

Bembem heard a noise and turned to see what it was. Two girls from the opposing team were crying foul over the goal. All the players rushed in, and a heated argument broke out.

'This was just a trial. Let's play the real game now,' the girl in the red jersey said.

'OK, let's play then,' someone from the opposition shouted back at her.

The girl held her head high.

'Let's toss first,' she said in a familiar voice. 'Everything is a toss of the coin.'

And she tossed Bembem's coin up in the rain.

The girl in red was Ima.

MAGIC

A bright ray of light peeked through the window curtain and woke Bembem up. The rain had stopped. Remembering her last night's dream, she thought it was the strangest she ever had. *Imagine Ima playing football! It's a maku-mang, for sure! So odd. But all dreams are odd, aren't they?*

Bembem then came out to the courtyard and looked for her father. However, he was nowhere to be seen.

Baba went to the hospital every two or three days but never so early. Feeling guilty for not giving him a proper answer last night, Bembem was determined to apologize as soon as he was back.

She saw Bobok tending to the chives at the kitchen garden and walked up to her.

'Oh, you are awake,' said Bobok. 'Your father has gone to the hospital.'

'Was he angry with me? Why did he leave so early? Is something wrong with Ima?' Bembem asked anxiously.

'No, my child. Why do you worry so much? He has gone to meet the doctor and will be back soon. Now, tell me, what are you wearing for the Thabal Chongba? Come, let's go in and start preparing for tonight.'

Bobok took out Bembem's mapaan-naiba phanek and blouse from the steel almirah. It was a sana-phige, the colour of gold.

Her velvet blouse was red and embellished with tiny golden leaves. They both agreed the attire would dazzle under the lights.

'Mother! Mother! Bem! Bembem!' It was Baba, calling from the courtyard. 'Bring out the fire.'

Without saying anything to Bembem, Bobok left the room hurriedly. She took the newspaper and the matchbox kept at the threshold of the main door, lit the newspaper, and carried it to the courtyard.

'May this fire cleanse you of all misfortunes,' said Bobok, putting the newspaper down on the ground, in front of Baba. Turning to the house, she called out in a voice cracked with emotions, 'O Bembem, my dear child, look, who's here!'

Bembem was upset that she was not informed of her mother's homecoming. Ima had been waking and slipping into *deep sleep* now and then for the past one month. The doctors could

neither find out why nor guarantee it would not happen again. To protect Bembem from any disappointment, her parents had decided it was better to keep the young child away from this new development. Four days ago, Ima had woken up again. This time, except for sleeping at nighttime, she didn't go back to her *deep sleep* again. One of the nurses noticed that Ima woke up from her last *deep sleep* just when the full moon of Yaosang was seen on the horizon.

Ima lay on the bed with Bembem. Gently patting her head, she explained the events at the hospital. After which, she said, 'Anyway, I heard you are a grown-up girl now. Baba told me of some of your adventures. I would love to hear more. Why don't you tell me what you did this Yaosang?'

With animated gestures, Bembem narrated everything; everything, except for her dreams. Ima listened with a serene smile and asked, 'Now, tell me, why is the coin so important to you?'

Bembem thought of telling Ima of the dreams too, but everything was fine and normal again. Her mother had returned home. There was no need to talk of confusing and strange things.

'It has a football etched on one side,' Bembem simply said. 'I have never seen a coin like that and you know how much I love football.'

Ima gave Bembem a surprise look and asked her to fetch Ima's old green bag.

Matchboxes, knives, screwdrivers, filed documents, and the green bag—these were the things Bembem was usually forbidden from playing with. The other things, she could understand why. But the faded green, nearly torn bag had always intrigued her.

She fetched the bag and handed it to Ima. Ima took out something from the inner pocket. As Bembem went closer, Ima opened the palm of her hand weakly.

'Is this your coin?' Ima asked.

It was! Bembem took the coin from Ima. She was in a daze when Baba came in and asked what Ima wanted for dinner.

'I don't know about dinner but I have a strong craving for ripe red silverberries with a bit of salt and lots of red u-morok!' replied Ima excitedly.

The coin dropped from Bembem's hand.

After the initial surprise, Ima recounted how the coin came into her possession.

'When I was of your age, my father, your late grandfather, brought two coins home one day. Just as you do, I loved to play football and would spend all my afternoons playing with friends...'

'WHAT! HOW! Wow! I would have never guessed you as a footballer!' Bembem couldn't believe her ears.

'Oh my! Is it that surprising? Now, let me continue,' Ima said with a laugh.

'Our field was beautiful and vast with a huge peepal tree on its edge. Whenever we were tired, we would lie down in the shade of the tree and look at the clouds above. In summer, we would bring green chillies and salt from home, plucked mangoes growing near the field, and eat them together.

'I still can't believe you played football. But why did you stop?'

'Do you know that big shopping complex? That's where our football field was. When construction for the complex began, I stopped playing. Going to another field and playing there was never the same. I was in love not just with football, but playing with friends on the green grass under the blue sky.'

Bembem loved her football field and could not imagine what Ima must have felt. She thought she should not talk about football with Ima anymore for the day. However, she hadn't got the answer to her mysterious coin.

'What happened to the other coin?' asked Bembem.

'I gave it to my coach as a gesture of respect.' All of a sudden, Ima seemed to be startled and said, 'Wait! You never told me who gave you the coin. You just said it was your nakatheng.'

'I didn't tell you because I went to the other side of the river for nakatheng. I know I am not supposed to go outside our leikai. I was scared that you might scold me.'

'What! Did you get it from that abandoned house?'

'Yes, an old woman gave it to me. She said I remind her of someone she knew. Do you know who she is?'

'I think I do! She is Bibi Maibam! But it is impossible!'

Bibi Maibam turned out to be Ima's coach. After becoming a doctor, she had left Manipur a long time ago. Ima often passed by Bibi's ancestral home, but never saw any sign of habitation. With all her family members gone for decades, the house had been abandoned. Thinking of the decrepit structure, overgrown with wild shrubs, Ima found it hard to believe that Bibi was back and living there once again.

At the revelation of these odd coincidences, Bembem decided it was time she told Ima of her strange dreams. After recounting everything, Bembem asked, 'Am I possessed, Ima?'

A moment of silence followed, and Ima finally spoke. 'No, my child. You will experience unexplainable situations in your life. Sometimes, there is no answer at all, but we should not let them bother us too much. Life is like that. Think of everything that happened in a positive light. The search for the coin introduced you to many new experiences. You went to the market on your own and came back safely, participated and won the tug of war game, made your own decisions, found new friends, and, of course, tasted u-morok for the first time! You are growing into your own person. That's why Baba and I can now proudly proclaim that you are a big girl. It's not possession, Bembem. Call it...magical!'

Ima kissed Bembem's forehead and calmed her down.

Bembem clutched onto Ima's coin all the while.

Fluorescent tube lights illuminated the decorated ground. Children and young people of all ages were standing in groups, ready to dance at the Thabal. Ahanbi was also standing at the entrance to the ground. Resplendent in a blue mapaan-naiba phanek, a matching blouse, and a sheer silk phee, she looked just like Saikhom Kamala, Bembem's favourite star.

Bembem was gazing at Ahanbi when Meme came up to her.

'What happened to your red velvet blouse?' Meme asked in surprise. 'Didn't we agree to wear matching blouses?'

'My velvet blouse doesn't have pockets,' replied Bembem.

'Why do you need a pocket?'

'For the...COIN! LOOK!' Bembem took out the coin from her blouse pocket and showed it to Meme.

'What? How? Is this some kind of magic?'

Takita takita takit
Dhong-ta takita
Takita takita takit

Drums for the Thabal Chongba started playing on the loudspeaker.

'No, it isn't magic. The magic is that Ima came back home today!' shouted Bembem.

'What?! That is such great news!' Meme gasped.

'Come, Meme, let's dance to this magical Yaosang!' said Bembem, pulling Meme by the hand and running towards the ground. Tonton trotted along.

Takita takita takit
Dhong-ta takita
Takita takita takit

GLOSSARY

leikai: loosely translated as locality or neighbourhood

phanek: Meitei women's traditional lower garment, stitched horizontally in the middle and worn like a sarong

phee: Meitei women's traditional upper garment, worn like a scarf or a shawl.

singju: a savoury and spicy side-dish or snack made of finely chopped seasonal vegetables, fermented fish called *ngaari,* roasted and grounded perilla seeds, chilli powder, among other condiments.

naahong: a woven cotton-cloth in white, specially used to carry babies on the back.

da/ dada: brother

che/ cheche: sister

maibi: Maibi has many roles in the traditional Meitei culture and society. Among others, they are traditional healers and priestesses.

Halangkar: Halangkar is celebrated on the fifth day of Yaosang, especially by the Hindu Meiteis. It is a reenactment of the Holi play between the lords Shri Govinda and Shri Bijoy Govinda. According to ancient Meitei belief, this day is related to 'Lai Keithel Kaba', roughly translated as 'when the gods held markets'. (refer to https://e-pao.net/epSubPageExtractor.asp?src=manipur.Arts_and_Culture.Shri_Bijoy_Govinda_Halangkar_Cultural_History_Of_Manipur_By_Ch_Jamini)

Brajamai: Goddess Radha's attendants in the Halangkar performance (refer to https://e-pao.net/epSubPageExtractor.asp?src=manipur.Arts_and_Culture.Shri_Bijoy_Govinda_Halangkar_Cultural_History_Of_Manipur_By_Ch_Jamini)

SOMETHING BORROWED: DIDA'S SARIS TO THE RESCUE

Madhumita Gupta

A NOTE BY THE AUTHOR

When I think about it, I feel this story grew from the stacks of neatly ironed saris I'd seen in the steel almirahs of my mother, her mother—my Dida, Mami and Mashi as a child. I'd marvelled at the sheer number initially, and then, when I grew up—the variety. And now, after I inherited many of those saris, it brings a big smile to my lips when I realize that these saris will never go out of style! Why? Because almost all of them are traditional styles rooted in the regions they were designed first. All the types of saris in the story have a strong background which keeps them heads and shoulders above transitional 'fashionable' saris.

The other strand of the story comes from my memories of the fun we had at weddings. Settled in Rajasthan I didn't get to see too many Bengali weddings and I loved meeting various relations and really enjoyed seeing the difference in customs—'shubho drishti' for one, is such a beautiful custom. Mishti, in my story, gave me the opportunity to revisit those customs and showcase it for you, the reader. I hope you will enjoy reading about these as much as I've enjoyed writing about them.

Bringing both these strands together was the idea that came from going back to simpler times when weddings were about families and friends getting together to celebrate the occasion, rather than the showy display of wealth that it has become. I remembered a news report about a young couple who had got married in a refreshingly simple ceremony and wished how lovely it would be if that could start a new trend! Chumki, in my story, does just that.

So, 'Something Borrowed' has been borrowed from multiple places—memories from my childhood, weddings then and now but above all, with a sincere wish to tell you a little about our traditions and of course, our saris!

THE UNEXPECTED ANNOUNCEMENT

Mishti, Ma, Baba, and Chotu are in the verandah as usual—the elders with their tea, Mishti with her Horlicks milk, and Chotu with his dog biscuit.

Ma insists on this 'quiet hour' every morning when the family sat in silence, sipping or crunching in Chotu's case, and took in the morning calm of the holidays.

However, the quiet is suddenly broken by a huge 'ishshsh' from Ma. The sound made Chotu cock an ear and look at her in alarm.

Ma is staring at her phone open-mouthed as her revered cup of tea lies untouched on the table by her two Nice biscuits.

'I really should not have broken my rule of not checking messages before tea...' she sighs rather pointedly and shakes her head.

'Uhm,' Baba is forced to lower the newspaper behind which he disappeared for at least half an hour every morning. 'What happened?'

'Don't ask!' Ma scowls. 'Today's children! It never happened in our times!'

Baba waits patiently. He and Mishti know too well that 'don't ask' meant 'don't ask, but I am going to tell you all about it in the tiniest detail'.

Sure enough, the story comes out the next minute.

Debolina-di, better known as Chumki-di, Mishti's older maashi's—Boro Maashi's—daughter, has decided to 'tie the knot' next month.

'Tie the knot?' Mishti visualizes sailors' knots and macrame knots which Dida, her grandmother, was teaching her last summer.

'It means getting married, Mishti,' Ma explains knowing Mishti's fertile imagination too well.

'Married? Chumki-di is getting married?' Mishti stares and then gets over her shock. 'What fun!'

'Fun?' Ma says. 'Not just married, married on the nineteenth. That's less than a fortnight...how will everything get done?'

'Everything will sort itself out,' Baba says comfortingly, but that seems to have the opposite effect and results in Ma sending him a dark look.

'Easy for you to say,' she scowls. 'So, so much to do, in such little time!' She resumes her complaining. 'Just like kids these days!'

Just then her phone rings stridently.

'That's Maashi,' she peers over her glasses.

'*Hainnn, bolo*!' and then starts a litany about kids these days.

Later, she tells Baba and Mishti the whole story. Chumki had met her knight in shining armour, Mohit Khatri, at the company she used to work for. They had dated and, within a couple of years, they had decided to marry. The reason they were marrying in a hurry was because Mohit had just been offered a wonderful job in Chicago, and they wanted to be married before he left. Since they had to move almost immediately, they had less than a month in hand.

'Well, we have to go to Kolkata as soon as you can get the tickets,' she looks at Baba, 'Others are also getting there by next week...'

And then she relapses into 'How will Dolly manage everything so quickly?'

Baba, Mishti, and Chotu clear out as quietly and quickly as possible before she can start over again.

The next two days are a flurry of activity as Ma races from room to room, almirah to almirah finding 'appropriate' clothes for the occasion. Only, nothing seems appropriate as she keeps complaining that she has worn all her special saris on different occasions.

'Tultul!' Baba finally bursts out. 'How in the world does it matter? Do you think anybody will remember what you wore during a wedding that happened five years ago?'

Ma subsides. She stops complaining but her rootling in the almirahs continues, along with trying different dresses on the unwilling model, Mishti.

'Uff!' Mishti moans as she takes off the nth dress she had tried. 'Ma I do not fit into that kurti any longer!'

The kurti joins the mountain of clothes on the bed—a mountain of her fancy-schmancy dresses.

'Or...' Mishti decides to try her luck picking up a pink and black sari from the mountain, 'I could wear this...'

Ma snatches it from her hands even before the sentence is complete. 'Absolutely not!' She glares at Mishti. 'You're ten! A sari? Don't even think about it!'

'But...'

'As it is you keep stumbling and falling even in your frocks...a sari...my goodness...no!'

Mishti subsided.

'Nothing to do then,' Ma declares, 'your Cinderella frock will have to be it.'

Truth be told, she did not like the pale blue shimmery Cinderella frock as much as she had a year ago. It was nothing like Meher's beeyootiful shimmery sharara or Tisha-didi's sari! Mishti longs to wear what she now knows is called 'ethnic'.

The other day when Ma was away at college, Mishti had tried out her saris in front of the mirror and LOOVED what she saw! Okay, maybe it wasn't draped and pleated perfectly. But she still looked good. Especially when she had worn one with high heels.

Weren't weddings the best occasions for wearing saris? If there is time, maybe she could coax Ma to buy her one later in Kolkata. *No chance*, Mishti shakes her head, what is she thinking?

She simply can't understand why Ma is being so difficult about a tiny thing like that.

TO KOLKATA

Eventually, the suitcases are all packed, and they are on their way to Kolkata. After the flurry of activity at the airport—Baba's multiple reminders of 'You do have your backpack, Mishti?', getting the boarding passes, check-in, and security (phew)—they are finally at Gate 4.

As they wait to board, Mishti's questions start like a bursting dam.

'Ma, I have never been to a Bengali wedding!'

'Is it very different from the ones we have been to?'

'Do they have sangeet and haldi, too?'

'Will we have to dance like at Neha-didi's wedding?'

'What?' Ma looks surprised. 'Oh, of course! You haven't attended any Bengali wedding!'

Mishti nods trying to look sad but not quite succeeding. She's too excited to be sad!

'Hmm, let's see!' Ma muses 'It is a bit different from North Indian weddings, though we are all adopting each other's customs now…but no, no dancing baratis still in Bengali marriages, certainly not at Chumki's...'

'Oh, it was different in our day!' Baba joins the conversation with something like a grimace turned into a grin. 'There was a more personal touch! You know, the weddings were at homes if they were big enough or in marriage homes. They were nothing like these elaborate weddings with wedding planners and what not!' he shudders. 'No substance, only style, if you ask me!'

Everybody knows how much Baba dislikes what he calls 'School Annual Day' weddings. 'All because of Bollywood,' he says disapprovingly. 'Choreographed dances, film star dresses, and what not! Jaataaa!'

Mishti doesn't quite agree. She loves the whole 'band baja baraat' spectacle!

But before she can go into that, Baba has time-travelled to his wedding. 'The menu, for starters!' His eyes become dreamy and he starts describing the extensive menu. 'Aah! The malai-chingri melted in your mouth!' He smacks his lips. 'And then there were three kinds of chops, oh, and the Bengali biryani, koraishootir kochuri, aloor dom, mishti doi, *and* channar jilipi...aah, what a feast it was!'

'Do you remember the ceremonies at all?' Ma begins laughing. Suddenly, she looks very young. Her eyes become starry at the memories of her wedding day. 'Or were you focused only on the food?'

'Of course, of course, I do remember the ceremonies,' Baba counters, but just then boarding is announced.

The whole journey, Ma determinedly tells Mishti about the various ceremonies in a Bengali wedding and their significance.

'I didn't quite want to write an essay on Bengali customs,' Mishti wants to tell her but then she looks at Ma's animated face and puts on *her* 'interested' face. Ma doesn't need more than the occasional 'Oh, reaaally?', 'Achcha?', and 'Wow!' to go on about the topic.

She's more interested in marvelling at the woolly meadow of clouds just below and the various shapes there.

She is listening with only half an ear till she hears the word 'games'.

'There's one where the wedding rings are dropped in a shallow vessel of milk...' Ma twinkles at Baba.

'Your Ma started cheating right then,' Baba smiles.

'I didn't! You were slow!'

'He's saying that because I found the ring first,' Ma laughs.

'Found?' Mishti is smiling too. 'Where?'

'There is a deep dish of milk,' Baba explains, 'in which the rings are dropped, and the bride and groom have to look for them!'

'It's funny,' Baba frowns. 'I had scanned the vessel very systematically with my fingers, and you were just splashing around. Yet you found them first!'

Mishti catches Ma's stifled giggle that becomes a little cough and looks at her startled. As Baba turns to the attendant, Ma puts her fingers on her lips. 'Later,' she mouths.

'Uhm, what was that?' Mishti knows Ma can be crafty! Had she cheated all those years ago? Perfectly possible!

'How come I'd never heard these stories before now?' Mishti asked as she trundled her Spiderman trolley towards the exit.

Will Chumki-di's wedding be as fun?

BIYE BAARI (THE WEDDING HOME)

If Ma and Baba's wedding day was what they called 'chaotic', Maashi's house is a jungle—everything was completely topsy-turvy when the Sens finally entered the imposing gates of the bungalow on Rashbehari Avenue. It resembled a grand mansion.

'One of the few bungalows still holding out against the invasion of high-rises!' Ma looks up and gently fingers the leaves of the old jasmine vine on the bamboo trellis at the entrance. Mishti is impressed too, but then she sees someone at the door.

Her oldest, best friend in the whole wide world! She starts running and almost knocks her grandma over in her excited hug.

'Dida!'

'Look at you!' Dida hugs her back warmly and laughs as she kisses the top of Mishti's head. 'Another year or two and you'll be taller than me!'

When they go inside, Mishti does a double take.

The place is teeming with people!

Whenever she had visited Maashi's place in the past, it had been just Maashi, Mesho, Dida, Chumki-di, and Bhuto-da. But now, it seems overcrowded with people of all shapes and sizes and ages all of whom seemed to know Ma and Baba!

All of a sudden, the three are surrounded by a horde of people! Mishti watched with wide eyes as various uncles affectionately slapped Baba on his back or hugged him and aunties kept coming and tousling Mishti's curls with shrieks of 'Oh! Isn't she a carbon copy of Tultul!'

And then start the baffling introductions:

'Mishti, this is Abha-di! You know Boro-di's niece?'

'Remember you met Matru-di when you were two?'

'The one sleeping on the sofa is Bhanu-da. He often gave you horseback rides on his back!'

How is Mishti supposed to remember all that?

Wherever you look, it is people and more people. Kakas,

mamas, dadas, didis, maashis, kakis... And suddenly Mishti finds herself standing all by herself as the flood of relatives take Ma and Baba away with them.

Dadu, Baba, and some Kakas stand arguing; Mamis sit chattering as they sort things and send the Dadas and Didis on endless errands of fetching tea and 'mishti'—desserts—which any Bengali will have at any time of the day!

Mishti realizes she is the youngest. Is there anyone at all her age in this bustling biye baari? She hasn't found a companion. *Yet*. It is boring, but if she got along with a bunch of didis and dadas...that should be good enough for a few days.

There are new people on the scene—the men who have come to construct the tent, holler as they erect awnings in the drive and the huge front yard; the florists are running around with armfuls of garlands; three plump ladies have taken over the kitchen as they wait for the rest of their team to arrive; light men run around with coils of fairy lights.

'Let me introduce Mishti to my friends,' exclaims Chumki-di, startling Mishti as she bounces up to her and catches her off guard.

Dida intervenes and rescues the bewildered Mishti. 'Let the kid take a breath!' and she whisks Mishti off to her room on the first floor.

She hears Ma complaining to her youngest sister's daughter. 'Chumki, just like you, springing a surprise wedding on us...'

Dida pushes open the door of her room. Thankfully, it is quiet and redolent of sandalwood incense, just like Mishti remembers it.

But wait...

A TRIP DOWN MEMORY LANE

The room may smell the same, but Mishti feels like she has stepped inside a shimmery rainbow. Instead of the neat bedcover, tucked very precisely at the corners, there is a heap of saris on the antique four-poster bed!

Except for in sari shops, Mishti has never before seen so many saris in one place—cotton saris, silk saris, God-knows-what saris in every colour present in Mishti's crayon box and even more.

'What is all this, Dida?'

'Ahh,' Dida sighs sadly, 'this is your Chumki-di's doing...'

'Eh?'

'You do know how quickly Chumki and Mohit decided to get married?'

'Oh yes!'

Mishti knows too well—her house had been turned upside down rummaging for wedding-worthy clothes! And that was followed by browsing through online stores to see whether those options were worth the price!

'Well, she didn't give anyone the time to buy new...' Dida pauses. 'What do they call them? "Ensembles"? They do have time to buy some things online but...can I tell you a secret?'

'Secret?' Mishti's eyes sparkle. She loves secrets! And then Dida lets Mishti in the BIG secret!

Ma and all three Maashis had turned to Dida and her famous treasure trove of saris—each lovingly preserved since forever.

'Oh, they drove me mad with their "please, please, please, Ma"!'

Dida said that they pestered her to lend her saris to everyone for the wedding.

'I am not too happy with this. Knowing how careless people can be these days, what if someone spills something or tears the fabric...' Dida shudders. She is very, very fond of her things, Mishti knows.

'I know,' Mishti interrupted. She imagines giving away her favourite T-shirts. 'I don't like lending my clothes. Not even the ones I no longer wear!'

Mishti wondered if her cousins would prefer Dida's saris over their amazing lehengas. She highly doubted that.

'Yes, you do get it!' Dida said. I know the girls aren't happy with losing the chance to go on shopping sprees...but I do hope they do that online thingy and leave my saris alone!'

She plopped down on the bed and continued. 'On the other hand, call me old-fashioned or just old but I never quite see the point of spending lakhs and lakhs just for a day or two!'

'That's a lot of money!' Mishti's eyes widened 'Lakhs?'

'Of course!' Dida said, nodding her head vigorously. 'When Manini's grandson got married, his bride's lehenga cost about a lakh! And how many times will she wear it in her entire life!'

'Well, it does seem like a waste.' Mishti agreed. 'Ma makes me wear the same things over and over again.'

'And then....' Dida started and stopped again.

'What?' Mishti prodded.

'Ah well...' Dida began a little haltingly. '...I am not going to wear all of these too often now and, if I take the time to sort through the saris, it would give me a chance to go through these cherished possessions of mine.'

Dida caressed a lovely red sari beside her. 'Since I took these out, I feel I am sifting through my memories, Mishtu!' Dida said quite poetically. 'And all except my wedding sari have been worn well and often!'

She picked up a radiant white and maroon sari and draped it around Mishti's shoulders.

'Mmmmmm! How soft!' she sighed and asked 'Is this a special sari?'

There was a dreamy smile on Dida's soft face 'It is, Mishtu! It is a Benarasi sari and this real gold zari, see?' she said, touching the intricate gold embroidery.

'Wait, let me show you something.'

Dida got up from the bed, pulled out a vintage album from the almirah, and flipped it open. It had black and white pictures of a wedding.

The faces of the couple exchanging garlands in the sepia picture looked familiar. Mishti peered hard.

'Is this you and Dadu?' she asked finding it very hard to believe that the very young, shy bride in the picture could be this very stern-ish Dida beside her.

Mishti was entranced and tickled!

'How funny!' she squealed with delight. 'I know the cameras on my parents' phones better than them and click pictures all the time! And here fifty or so pictures are capturing the whole event!'

'And yet nothing has been left out. Everything from my gaaye holud to the bou-bhaat is in this album. And all the people in our lives!'

It became even more fun when Dida told Mishti the stories behind the beautiful saris she and the people in the photographs were wearing! Mishti was a hoarder herself, but to be able to preserve saris from so long ago and ensure they remain in excellent condition was unbelievable!

'You know, I just realized that at least in one way, Chumki's wedding and mine are similar to each other.' Dida said. 'After nearly half a century, a wedding is taking place in a house!'

Just then the door opened and Ma came in wiping her hands! 'Oof this Chumki…' she began and her eyes fell upon the mountain of saris and the wedding album.

'Oh my God! Your wedding album, Ma!' she exclaimed, grabbing the album and plopping down on the bed. 'It is your shubho drishti!' she said with a look of adoration at Dida.

'Will somebody tell me what all these customs mean?' Mishtu interjected.

'In a minute!' Dida said and turned to Ma. 'Can you tell me the one big similarity between Chumki's wedding and mine?'

'Huh?' Ma's brows crinkled up as she tried to think.

Mishti giggled and wiggled, finding it hard to contain herself, and then she burst out before Ma got a fair chance: 'They are both getting married in an actual home, Ma!'

So true! All the weddings Mishti had been to, were at 'marriage homes', havelis, and heritage hotels. This is what had struck her very odd when she had arrived that morning—a home had been transformed into the wedding venue. But how nice it was! Loud and crazy, yes, but so very nice.

CHUMKI TEACHES MISHTI AN IMPORTANT LESSON

'What is happening here?' Mishti asks, as she flipped a page and saw Dida, the very young Dida, being carried by four handsome men who were laughing delightedly.

'My Mamas!' Ma looked again. 'How young you all were! Here, Dida is being carried on a wooden plank by her brothers for the shubho drishti.'

'And what is shubho drishti?' Mishti asked again patiently.

'It is supposed to be the first time the bride and groom see each other,' Dida explained. 'Hence, there is a betel leaf in front of my face in this picture!'

'You hadn't met Dadu before that day?'

Mishti couldn't begin to imagine such a thing! Look at Chumki-di finding her groom all by herself! Mishti intended to do just that if and when she wanted to get married!

'Oh, times have changed since then!' Dida laughed at Mishti's surprised expression. 'But no, your Dadu and I had met earlier. We were actually neighbourhood friends. Shubho drishti is just a very sweet, romantic custom!'

'It is that indeed,' Ma sighed, maybe remembering her own shubho drishti. 'And it is such an affectionate gesture from your brothers and cousins. Maybe also a symbol of bye-

bye to all the pampering at the girl's father's house?'

'Who will carry Chumki-di?' Mishti thought of her plump sister and was ready to pity the poor people who might have to carry her!

'All your dadas I guess.' Dida smirked as well. Maybe she was also thinking the same thing!

Ma instantly caught the look that had passed between the grandma and the grandchild. 'Both of you are quite mean, you know!' she said reproachfully. 'Chumki is going to be the sweetest bride ever.'

'Absolutely! Sweetest and solidest!' Mishti quipped.

Mishti was so busy looking at the pictures that she had completely failed to hear the door open and Chumki enter the room. The soon-to-be bride had quietly come inside and was standing right behind her!

When a deep voice said 'Uhhm!' right behind her left ear, Mishti jumped violently!

Chumki leapt on Mishti and tickles her mercilessly till she was laughing helplessly and rolling all over the bed!

'Stop it, Didi. Stop it!' Mishti screamed.

'Stop it! Stop it!' Dida also yelled. 'My beautiful saris... you're crushing them all!'

Chumki stopped and Mishti sat up, wiping her eyes. 'You're cruel, Chumki-di!'

'Achcha?' Chumki answers with a mocking scowl. 'I wonder who was body shaming me just now!'

'Body shaming?' Mishti asked. She didn't know what that was.

'Making fun of or commenting on somebody's physical appearance is a strict no-no, Mishti,' Chumki-di explained in a serious voice.

'So, no calling you "solid"?'

'No. And certainly not in front of Mohit!'

Chumki turned to Dida. 'Why have you got all these saris out, Didu?'

It was Dida's turn to become secretive. 'No reason,' she said turning away and hiding a smile.

In a clear tactic to change the topic, Mishti said rather loudly, 'Oh look, these photographs are in colour!' and she flipped to the end of Dida's album to show everyone the pictures that were not black and white.

'This is your mother's gaaye holud,' Dida answered with a smile. 'But the pick of the lot is this...I bet no one can forget this historical day!'

She skipped a few pages, reaching one where many people were sitting around a mammoth dining table and laughing uproariously. At the head was Mishti's mother, looking young and...decidedly sheepish!

Mishti was intrigued.

'What happened here?' she asked. 'Why is Ma looking like that?'

Just then the door opened and Baba and Dadu came in.

'Phew!' Baba throws himself on the couch, 'It is total bedlam out there!'

'Obviously,' Dadu beamed. 'What else did you expect at a biye baari?'

Just then his eyes fell on the album. 'Aha! Your favourite pastime!'

'Look, Mishti. Wasn't I handsome?' Dadu pointed at the groom in a picture.

'You! No way it's you!' said a shocked Mishti, looking at the person in the picture and then shifting her gaze to Dadu who was standing in front of her.

Dida winked. 'Who would believe your Dadu was such a dashing young man?'

'He had hair on his head!' Mishti could barely believe it was her Dadu in the photograph. He looked like a film star. And ever since she could remember Dadu's head has been as bald as a football! He even let Mishti play tabla on his head sometimes!

Baba flips through the pages, and he too stops at the very same picture Dida and Mishti had been looking at.

'You remember your daughter's bou-bhaat?' he asked Dida with a laugh.

'Don't I?'

And then the story of the auspicious first meal—the bou-bhaat— was revealed. Ma had made daal and payesh.

'The payesh was superb,' Baba said. But the daal...well...it was just litres and litres of pale, yellow water with some onions floating bleakly in it...' He could barely complete the sentence before collapsing with laughter. 'I remember thinking to myself that I'm done for...'

'It's a good thing that you were a skilled cook, Ashish,' Dida says. 'When I think about it, I should have taught Tultul at least some basic cooking—it is nothing less than a critical life skill!'

'I think I share the blame too,' Dadu joins, wiping his eyes. He had been laughing so hard that he had tears in them. 'Tultul was my baby, and I thought cooking was beneath her! I was very wrong, and as your Dida said, cooking IS one of the most essential life skills.'

'Even your Dadu can cook a bit now,' Dida chimed in. 'And with Ashish's help, our daughter is a pro now. She has come a long way!'

It was difficult for Mishti to imagine her mother as ever being poor at cooking. She thought Ma was the best cook in the world. But after hearing the story of the bou-bhaat she decided to learn from Ma so she would never end up making a litre of yellow water.

'I am rather proud of my mutton curry and matar paneer, if I may say so myself,' Baba preens. 'Learn enough to survive, I say!'

'Or find a good cook!' suggests Chumki who was famous for her dislike of cooking.

That sounded like an infinitely better idea to Mishti.

Dida, Dadu, and Baba continue to explore the album and tell Mishti many more stories behind the pictures. It felt like travelling through time. And marvel of marvels—Dida remembered the history and memories attached to every sari they spotted in the photographs.

'And with this,' Dida picked up a bold olive green sari with beautiful detailing all over, 'the next generation arrives!'

'Wow! It's like the whole of the *Jungle Book* out here!' Mishti stared goggle-eyed at the sari before her. She peers closely and lists all the birds and animals she can find in the embroidery. 'Peacocks, flowers, trees, and what's this? A hut and cow? Wow!

'Ma, don't you have a similar something in a lighter colour?' she asked.

'All my daughters have these "Kantha" sarees,' beamed Dida.

'Kantha? Is that a place?' Mishti asked.

'No, no!' Dida and Ma laughed. 'Guess again.'

Mishti shook her head. 'Is it a kind of sari?'

'Yes, it is now,' Ma nodded. 'But it wasn't so originally.' She turned to Dida 'Ma, why don't you tell her the story of Kantha?'

'I can do one better!' Dida answered and, the next minute, she pulled out a somewhat discoloured tablecloth-ish thing with similar embroidery from the depths of her almirah.

'This,' she said spreading the cloth on the bed, 'Mishtu, is your original Kantha!'

'What? Mine?'

'When you were only a month old,' Dida said, 'you and your mom were here for a couple of months, and this is one of the kanthas I made for you!'

'What? Why?'

'Er...so that you didn't soil my bedsheets!' Dida said with a grin.

Everyone burst out laughing looking at Mishti's surprised face.

'You know,' Ma continued 'instead of fancy crib sheets and swaddles, we preferred sheets that are stitched at home for newborns...'

'This was once a sari, a cotton one that could be worn daily and washed over and over for this gossamer softness, making it just right for a baby's soft bottom,' Dida says with a twinkle in her eyes as Mishti's face went red.

'And all this hard work just to soak up the baby's you-know-what!' Mishti says, running her hands over the embroidery.

'This is not as hard as it looks,' Dida said as she brought out her sewing kit. 'Let me show you.'

She deftly threads a needle with some red thread and then picks up a pencil. On a white piece of cloth, she swiftly draws a flower and then her needle flies in and out around that flower. Within a few minutes, the embroidered red flower stood in all its glory in a corner of the white cloth.

'You can do it too, Mishti,' Dida said, threading a green thread and drawing a pair of leaves under the flower. 'Here let me show you how to do this running stitch.'

It took Mishti a while but soon enough there were two leaves under the flower.

'Wow!' she felt so proud of her handiwork, 'Draw something else or let me do it!'

Dida happily drew some more flowers and leaves to compliment the embroidery they had already done. This time, Mishti threaded the needle herself with a lovely blue thread. Within minutes, the white piece of cloth had transformed into a beautiful embroidered handkerchief with red and blue flowers in a bush of green leaves.

For a moment, Mishti beamed proudly. But then a frown appeared on her face. 'I still don't know why it's called a kantha.'

Dida picked up that old, old sheet again. 'This is a kantha—an old sari and cloth stitched together and then embroidered beautifully using a running stitch.'

'And then some designer picks the design up, puts it on silk, and claims they "invented" the fancy "Kantha" saris!' Ma added.

'And then make us pay thousands for something which was originally a baby's botty sheet!' Baba said with a laugh.

'Babaaa,' Mishti shouted, 'don't call it that!'

DIDA'S SARI STORE

Just then the door burst open and all the girls of the family trooped in like a flock of loud birds! Instantly the room was full of *oohs* and *aaahs*.

'My God! Look at that orange sari!' Abha-di squealed.

'Is that a kanjeevaram?' Runu-di had stars in her eyes as she held a sari which looks liked flowing gold.

Baba and Dadu looked at each other with alarm—now these girls will go on indefinitely about saris and the legends behind them. They knew the chain of events all too well. In a jiffy, they got up and escaped Dida's room as quickly as they could.

Dida wasn't aware that the maashis had started a casual rumour about Dida having enough saris for everyone in the biye baari. And it was this rumour which had brought all the young girls to Dida's room just when all of them were conveniently displayed on the bed!

'Didu!' Shipra-di said, grabbing a bright blue sari with gorgeous silver work all over, 'You have to, have to, have to let me wear this someday!'

'No way,' Dida looked horrified. 'Do you have any idea how much a real Paithani silk sari costs?'

The didis exchanged glances. The generation that lived in their jeans had no idea about saris, their heritage, or how expensive they were.

Mishti was curious too. But her knowledge of prices wasn't that good.

'A few thousand rupees?' she guessed.

Dida burst out laughing. 'Multiply that by twenty!'

Mishti was aghast 'Thhhhaaaat much!'

'How old are these saris, Thamma?' Mintu-di asked.

'Let's say *very* old!'

'Antiques!' Mishti quipped. She couldn't help showing off her new vocabulary.

'Indeed, they are antiques!'

'Heirlooms!' Chumki said picking up a silk sari in the most delicate shade of turquoise.

'Indeed, and so well preserved!' Mishti added.

'If we promise to take very good care of them, then can we borrow them someday?' Abha-di was holding a rich green sari in front of her and preening in the mirror.

'Please, please, please!' everyone joined in. 'PLEASE Dida!'

'OK, OK, you varmints!' Dida said softly. 'I guess I will have to let you take my saris...' she paused, '...after I'm dead and gone!'

Since Dida's attachment to her saris was legendary, everyone understood her sentiment.

'Don't you worry, Didu,' Chumki said soothingly, 'we're all ordering our saris online today itself...'

'But Maa!' Mishti's mother exclaims. She still looks aghast. 'Don't be so stingy. You've uncountable saris and yet...'

'That is how you have uncountable saris,' Dida smirked, happy that she wouldn't have to part with them.

'But I have just one request Dida, can I borrow this for just my aiburo bhaat?' Chumki asked picking up a pink jamdani sari.

'I guess...only because you're the bride...' Dida relented.

'But on ONE condition. You must return this in as pristine a shape as you're taking it!' Dida warned Chumki.

'Of course, Dida! 'I'll wear a bib when I'm eating in it!'

And before the other girls started getting ideas, Dida quickly began folding and putting away the saris.

SOME HOPE

The girls had left the room and Dida was just finishing folding her saris.

'Aaah!' Dida straightened herself finally and was surprised to see Mishti still in the room.

'Is aiburo bhaat something like bachelor parties?'

'It is indeed,' Dida replied. 'The only difference is that it is celebrated at home or homes...'

'Homes?'

'Yup, like today it will be at Boro Maashi's place, tomorrow it will be at Kaka's place and so on...'

'But everyone is here for Chumki-di's wedding?'

'And so, there will be one BIG aiburo bhaat here itself and we will all prepare her favourite food!'

'Ooh!' Mishti started drooling imagining the mountains of food that would be served!

And then her face fell. Soon everyone will be buying new saris online, wearing them for different occasions, and swishing their brilliant pallus like Bollywood stars, but Ma will make her wear a frock even though she is old enough to manage a sari.

Unknowingly, a great, big sigh escaped her.

Dida's antenna went instantly up. She had uncanny eyes and ears that caught anything amiss.

'Aah, no, nothing,' Mishti didn't quite want to tell tales about Ma being so horrendously stubborn about the frock. Why would one be so stubborn about such a little thing?

'Out with it!' Dida ordered. 'No secrets, that was our pact, remember?'

'I want to wear a sari, too, on Chumki-di's wedding day,' Mishti burst out. 'But Ma has brought along my Cinderella frock...and she will make me wear it...' She stopped and looked at Dida quizzically 'Unless...'

'Unless what?' Dida's eyes were beginning to shine like her favourite cat, Mini. She and Mishti had often hatched plans that the household had never heard about.

'There is a Plan B—will you help me?' Mishti's eyes twinkle.

And she launched into Plan B which she had thought about ever since. It will take some manoeuvring but it looked perfectly do-able.

'That sounds like a good plan!' Dida approved wholeheartedly. 'You try to get around that stubborn daughter of mine first...'

'And if that doesn't work' Mishti jumps down the giant bed 'Plan B!'

Dida nodded her head.

'There you are!' Dida exclaimed, finding Mishti in the middle of learning to French-braid her hair. She hurries her along to her room the next morning, saying, 'Get ready by 11 a.m., and don't tell anyone where we're going.'

Mishti was intrigued, 'Where are we going?'

Dida only smiled mysteriously and warned, 'You'll see. Don't eat too much!'

An hour later, Mishti was ready and had finished her breakfast when Dida, Ma, Boro Maashi, and Dadu tiptoed out of the house. Dadu drove them off in their old Santro, and Mishti felt special as the only young one on this secretive trip. After a half hour of searching for parking, Dadu dropped the others off at a sari shop in Gariahat, and he and Mishti finally found a spot near a green veranda where a lovely Labrador was playing with its owner. That's when Dadu revealed the surprise: they were shopping for gifts for everyone, especially the girls who couldn't shop themselves.

The market was a bustling wonderland, filled with everything from small pavement stalls to grand showrooms selling saris, clothes, jewellery, and knick-knacks. Maashi went wild picking out gifts like paintings, decorations, and a small Ganesha idol for Chumki to take with her when she moved to Chicago. Dida carefully selected thoughtful presents for all her grandchildren: silverware for Chumki's new home, a trendy lipstick for Abha-di, a brass Bankura horse for Runu-di, and a soft Corgi toy for Mishti herself, which Mishti could hardly contain her excitement over. After hours of shopping, the family, laden with bags, made their way to a famous restaurant, Bhojon Bahar, where they feasted on biryani, garlic noodles, chole bhature, phuchkas, and chaats. Mishti was in food heaven. However, when they returned, the car seemed to have vanished! Panic set in, but thanks to Mishti's sharp memory of a green verandah and the friendly yellow Labrador there, she led Dadu to where he had parked the car, saving the day and avoiding a trip to the police pound. Everyone heaved a sigh of relief, grateful for Mishti's keen observation.

MOSTLY ABOUT A NEAT CONE!

'The idea!' Ma fumed 'Out of QUESTION!'

She was hauling a huge karahi from the usually locked-up storeroom looking extremely flustered.

'Wear a sari' she frowned darkly 'Indeed!'

Mishti scowled equally darkly 'But everyone else is wearing saris... Ma...?'

'You're too young!'

'But...'

'Mishti!' her mother said warningly, which was a clear sign that the conversation ended RIGHT HERE, RIGHT NOW.

Mishti stamped out fuming. It was such a simple, tiny request! Ma had no business getting so het up about that. After the shopping trip, Ma had been in a great mood especially as her gifts had been appreciated a lot and Mishti had thought that she might give in now...but of course not.

Mishti was delighted about her favourite didi's surprise wedding but EXTREMELY unhappy that her mother wouldn't let her wear a sari for even one of the many ceremonies. It seemed so unfair.

If Mishti wore her Cinderella dress from her tenth birthday, seven months ago, she felt she would stick out like a very sore thumb in that melee of colourful sari-clad didis.

Why couldn't Ma be reasonable?

It was time to enlist Dida's help for Plan B.

Determined, she made her way to Dida's room through the heaps of wedding stuff that was strewn everywhere.

'Hey Mishti!' Chumki-di waylaid her just then. 'Where have you been hiding? You're to be my nitkone, you know?'

'Neat cone?' Mishti was instantly suspicious. 'What is that?'

'Not "neat cone", nitkone! It's like the bride's best girl!' Chumki-di laughed.

'Potato, potahtoe!' Mishti had recently learnt this new expression and was happy to practise it.

'Forget the potato, come, I'll show you your tatto!'

The word sounds terribly like a tattoo and a terrified Mishti tries to wrench her hand away. 'I don't want any tattoo!'

'Oh God! No,' Chumki started laughing again. 'Not tattoo, it is tatto, or tattva. Come you'll see, your favourite is in there.'

Now what? Weddings were so confusing! There were way too many rituals!

They entered Maashi's room, the largest one in the Roy mansion after Dida's room. And at the moment, also the noisiest.

The whole floor was strewn with beautifully decorated cardboard boxes. Maashis, mamis, kakis, and didis are neatly arranging new clothes, fruits, sweets, and what seemed like tonnes of make-up products...in the boxes...

'What IS all this?'

'This is usually done at the groom's home but since Mohit is not from Kolkata,' Mami explained, pointing to a lady arranging one of the trays, 'we told his mother there that we could do it here instead.'

'This is all for us!' Abha-di said. 'We're gift-wrapping our gifts!'

'And that is what "tattva" is—gifts from the groom's family to the bride and her family. And sometimes, it is vice versa,' Dida joined in.

'Where's mine?' Mishti perked up 'I'm the neat cone!'

'Neat cone?' Dida looked flabbergasted.

'She means nitkone!' Chumki collapses on the bed in a fit of laughter. 'Neat cone! Come here! See!'

Yes, it was another fluffy, sparkly frock!

Mishti's face fell even as she braved a smile. 'Oh! That's beautiful!'

Apparently, that was why Ma had suddenly disappeared during the shopping spree, to get her a new frock.

Mishti barely looked at the embellished jeans, the cat-print shirt, and the Frozen make-up stuff that were also in the box.

'Your mom said this was your favourite dress? You'll look lovely in it, and I can pretend Cinderella is my neat cone!' Chumki-di said.

Mishti was not amused, but she stole a glance at Dida.

She just had to talk to Dida. She was the only one who could help her.

Dida gave her a slight nod.

Her watchful eyes hadn't missed anything. She got up and said a little too loudly, a little too theatrically, 'Come, Mishti, let me show you something.'

Mishti was only too glad to follow her out of the room.

PLAN B

As they made their way to Dida's room, Mishti was wondering how Plan B was to work.

They made a detour to the kitchen—mouth-watering fragrances wafted from there. It smelt like koraishooti kochuri.

'Here,' Dida called imperiously, 'one nice big plate of kochuri and aloo sabji for my natni here!'

Maya-di, the fierce in-charge of the ever-busy kitchen, ladled out a generous plateful of golden, hot, crisp kochuris with steaming sabji. Mishti's spirits lifted immediately—who can sulk in front of such food? She held the plate carefully as she and Dida climbed the stairs to Dida's room where she licked the plate clean. Then they discussed Plan B.

And what a plan it was—simple but effective. Mishti crossed her fingers.

'Not a word to anyone though,' Dida warned. 'The grapevine works overtime here!'

Mishti knew what that meant.

'I know, Dida,' she nodded sagely. 'Rumours travel fast in this house, Abha-di was saying that she knew all about how the maashis were planning to lend your saris to the didis if required...'

'And now,' Dida looked despairingly out of the big window 'with this never-ending rain I think I will have no choice but to hand out my saris...'

'Isn't it good, Dida?' Mishti was puzzled. 'As it is, you rarely wear all those beautiful saris...'

'Be that as it may, but our plan has to be a secret between the two of us, okay?'

Mishti held out her little finger.

'What's that?' Dida looked surprised.

'Give me your little finger,' Mishti commanded and when Dida did that, she linked the two fingers together and said, 'Pinky promise! That's the strongest promise. Neither of us can break it now!'

'Ohh! We won't! Not unless you want to wear your Cinderella frock for the wedding.'

'Nooope!'

'Okay, close your eyes now.'

Aha! Mishti loved Dida's 'close your eyes' games! They generally ended with something totally unexpected in her lap. Her dear, dear Chotu had been one such 'close-your-eyes' gift on her eighth birthday. The shock of the small, tubby pup wiggling in her lap and sniffing excitedly around her had made Mishti jump up with excitement and instantly lose her heart to the cutest yellow Labrador pup! The two had been inseparable since then.

She heard Dida get up, the bunch of keys jangling, and the slight creak as she opened her almirah. She pulled something out and plonked it on Mishti's lap. The next moment Mishti was staring spellbound at the world's most gorgeous sari that Dida had! A deep, rich red silk sari with intricate, delicate gold patterns all over and a deep midnight blue border and pallu.

'I saved this Muga especially for you, Mishtu,' Dida smiles gently.

'WHAT! Are you sure that Ma...?'

'I'll handle her,' Dida says briskly. 'Not a word to anyone, it's our secret!'

Mishti does a little dance and envelops Dida in a bear hug.

CHUMKI'S I-BURP BHAAT

If the last couple of days had been a whirlwind of shopping and packing the tattvas, today was complete chaos! Since the previous afternoon, it had become dark and cloudy, but inside Roy's mansion, the mood was festive!

It was Chumki's aiburo bhaat that day, and everyone was in the kitchen. The kitchen, which on usual days, had looked huge, was bursting at seams that day. Everybody from Maya-di and Dida to all the maashis and kakis and mamis was present inside—each person was busy with chopping, slicing, stirring, and shouting! Since very early that morning, delicious aromas had been floating out from the kitchen. Mishti suddenly realized she was starving.

Here Boro Maashi was making Chumki's favourite bread rolls stuffed with spicy potato filling; Ma was making her famous halwa; and there; Choto Maashi was preparing her famous malai chingri for lunch. Baba had been allotted a corner, where he was completely absorbed in making paayesh in a huge pan and, of course, there was the usual happy confusion all around with people looking for their ingredients and blaming each other for stealing their khunti.

It had started raining and was gradually getting darker and darker.

'Do you think our saris can reach us in this terrible weather?' Runu-di gazed out disconsolately.

'I doubt it,' Ma said peeling some potatoes. 'But don't worry, if worst comes to worst...'

'Shhh, Di!' Choto Maashi shushed Ma immediately, and the girls exchanged a curious look.

'Oh, heh, heh,' Ma said lamely and tried to change the subject. 'I meant we will think of something, you just focus on stuffing yourself today heh...heh...'

'Can you imagine being able to eat all that?' Chumki giggled. She too had sneaked in.

'I think I could!' Mishti smacked her lips. 'Is it all for you only?'

'As if!' Chumki said. 'Of course, you being the "neat cone" get to enjoy the lion's share!'

'Aha! When, when?'

'Soon! Soon!'

'What does it mean, the word "aiburo bhaat"?'

'Okay, let's see,' Chumki explained. 'Aiburo bhaat signifies my last meal as an unmarried girl, seeing that it's my wedding soon.'

'So this is something like a bachelorette party,' Runu-di added, busily chopping almonds for the halwa.

'Only, it is with the family and by the family...'

And what a wonderful, wonderful ritual it turned out to be.

Chumki and Mishti, all bathed and dressed in new clothes sat on the floor as Dida had instructed.

'How beautiful Chumki-di is looking!' Mishti couldn't help gaping at her didi who was looking resplendent in a bright red sari—the only one which had arrived before the torrential rains of the morning which had made everyone doubt the success of their online shopping arriving in time.

Boro Maashi took turns between wiping her eyes with her pallu and feeding Chumki-di like a baby.

'Have you quite forgotten that Chumki is a fully qualified professor of Marketing?' Mesho teased Maashi when he saw that.

'I know, I know. But today she is my baby!'

Chumki-di, of course, was enjoying every bit of getting babied. She opened her mouth wide for every bite! Mishti smartly followed the lead, and let Ma feed her, her hands folded demurely on her lap.

Mishti refused the mandatory shukto—she couldn't understand how everyone else loved the bitter delicacy! But she tried everything else, from the bhaja moog daal, aloo and begun bhaja, kosha mangsho, luchi and aloor dom, malai chingri, and then the rosogollas and payesh. 'Team Kitchen' had outdone itself in both variety and quantity!

But guess what! Even after all this feeding, with Mishti almost bursting with food, she still couldn't resist the last spoonful of creamy payesh. And as opened her mouth, out came the BIGGEST BURP ever! It was so sudden and so loud that everyone looked up in astonishment.

'*Baap re baaap*!' exclaimed Baba and Mesho together, bursting into loud laughter. That of course, made everyone join in. How everyone laughed, making Mishti join in as well.

'That is one aiburo bhaat I'm never going to forget!' Dida said, wiping her tears.

'I'm going to call this our I-Burp Bhaat!' Chumki said, bursting into helpless laughter again.

BURRRPPP

ON TO PLAN B

'Get up, get up, Mishti!' Ma calls 'Big day today!'

'The wedding is still two days away?' Mishti sits up, rubbing her eyes.

'Not the wedding, Mohit is coming to meet us today!'

Of course! Mishti had completely forgotten about that. She jumps up. She had about a hundred questions. But first, she had to talk to Chotu—poor fellow, all alone, back in Jaipur.

She took Ma's phone and video-called Bimla-didi at home who dutifully held the phone in front of Chotu. His big grinning mouth and black eyes stared back at her somewhat confused when she called him 'Chotu! Chotu!'

'Is he eating well?'

'Are you brushing him every day?'

'Yes, didi,' Bimla sounded mildly offended. 'I take care of him like my own son!'

Mishti was satisfied though she still wished she could take Chotu everywhere.

'Come!' Ma called again. 'That's quite enough, get ready now!'

'What should I call him Ma? Is Mohit-da OK?'

Mishti couldn't call him Jija-ji or Jamai-babu like everyone else—too awkward!

When she saw him for the first time, standing in the middle of the giggling circle of the didis, she was totally blown over.

'Not that he is handsome like a film star,' she teased Chumki-di, 'but he's cute, and I like his big smile a lot!'

Mishti, the blabbermouth that she was, was tongue-tied when she was finally introduced to Mohit, but he was so charming that within minutes, they were chatting away like old friends!

Chumki-di looked on fondly 'She's my "neat cone".'

'Neat what?' Mohit asked.

It fell to Mishti to explain what a neat cone was.

Once she was over her initial self-consciousness, she had a hundred questions for Mohit. How did he meet Chumki? Where was he born? Does he like Bengalis? When will they leave for Chicago?

By the time her interrogation ended, Mohit had broken into a sweat. 'Now I know what an interrogation means.'

'That is what neat cone does!'

'Another few minutes of this, and I'd have run off without Chumki!'

Neither of them knew when Chumki had entered the room 'Really, Mohit?' she scowled.

'Mishti should become an investigator when she grows up!'

'Just one question for you Chumki-di.'

'What?'

'What do you like the most about Mohit?'

'Oh! I don't know...'

After some thought, Chumki answered with a smile, 'The one quality is that he's truly very kind and compassionate. Still want to run off without your bride?

'No, he won't,' Mishti said sagely. 'I've tested him, he'll do.'

'*He'll do*?' Now it was Mohit's turn to look offended.

'Yeah, yeah, you will!' Mishti laughed and ran off.

'What a precocious kid!' Mohit exclaimed with a chuckle.

'Nah!' Chumki defended her favourite cousin. 'She's cute.'

CONFUSION CONFOUNDED

'Wake up, Mishti!' Baba was poking at Mishti. 'We have to be down for breakfast soon!'

Mishti opens her eyes a crack and then sits up, staring outside in astonishment. She had never seen such pouring rain in her life.

'Aha! That might mean koraishootir kochuri...'

'Baba!' Mishti scolded. 'The saris were supposed to arrive today!'

She doubted if the courier service could brave the rains.

And true enough, all the didis downstairs looked as glum as the overcast skies.

Moreover, there were no kochuris to Baba's huge disappointment.

'Bread, butter, and eggs,' Ma said, putting the plates on the table. She looks worried too.

'Cheer up,' she said, more to convince herself than others. 'We have the whole day today, maybe the rain will stop...'

'Hah!' Chumki wailed, looking at her phone. 'There is a 100 per cent chance of rain today and tomorrow...and it's not even technically monsoon yet!'

Mishti looked at Dida, who was frowning. Mishti knew exactly what she was worried about.

'Well...' Mishti cleared her throat 'Uhm...I think Dida has something to say, don't you, Dida?'

Dida gave her an agonized look but nodded.

'Err...yes,' she looked again at Mishti, who nodded firmly. 'Yes, I do indeed. If worst comes to worst...you girls can borrow my saris for the wedding day...though I do hope the weather clears up, then there would be no need for them heh...heh...heh.'

The whole day passed with the didi's looking out of the windows and sighing.

'If only courier-wala's had boats,' Mishti tried to lighten the mood.

'Shut up, Mishti!' Chumki scolded her. 'No one is in the mood for jokes.'

Mishti sauntered off, a little annoyed and went to Dida's room.

'You want me to help take out your saris?'

'Go away, Mishti!' Dida said crossly, turning on her side.

Everyone was as glum and irritable as the weather. Mishti went and video-called Bimla-didi for Chotu—only he was smiling away as always.

It rained and rained. It was clear that it wasn't going to stop.

There was nothing to it, and after a silent dinner, the girls trooped up to Dida's room.

And Dida had no choice but to open her veritable sari shop.

DIDA'S DOKAAN

'Dida!' everyone's eyes became as big as Bheemsen and Co.'s roshogollas when they saw Dida's sari collection. 'You're a hoarder!'

'Well, I taught in a prestigious college,' Dida defended her beloved collection 'I had to dress well!'

'Dress well, indeed!' interjected Dadu, who had joined the fun. 'I suffered the never-ending trips to sari stores. The salespeople knew us by our names!'

'Okay girls!' Dida handed over her empire to Chumki. 'Feel free to take your pick. But. You have to return every one of them in perfect condition. OK?'

'YES!' they shouted together, and it became a free-for-all sale with squeals of 'Look at this! Gorgeous! Oh my God!'

While the maashis were *oohing* and *aahing* and apparently speaking Greek—Patola, Paithani, Bandej, Bagru, Benarasi, Muga, and Dhakai—it was the Jaamdaani saris that drew the biggest squeals of delight, right after the Kanjeevaram. The girls were speaking another language of colours: beige, fuchsia, burgundy, wine red, turquoise, amber, lavender, arctic, and so on. Teams from two generations looked astonished at the sheer variety of fabrics and colours.

And then began 'War of the Worlds 2'.

'Beige is my colour!'

'Not at all, it is for older people like us!'

'I'll take the lavender...'

'Nope, that Bandej is mine.'

Mishti had seen Baba and the uncles of the family peek in; no doubt, they were baffled about the commotion inside and then disappeared just as fast.

After about half an hour of spirited battle finally, the girls left with their booties, leaving only Chumki-di and Mishti with the aunties behind.

'*Baap re!*' Boro Maashi laughed. 'Those girls did put up quite a fight! But thank God! I got my Paithani!'

'Di,' Ma said a little too innocently. 'I wanted that one, but just once, I'll bow to your seniority.'

'Seniority? *Dekhachchi toke*!' and with that Maashi started pummelling Ma with a bolster.

Chumki and Mishti looked on astounded. Who would have imagined the staid ladies could indulge in a pillow fight?

Ma was so much fun here at the house. It was as if she had found her inner child again. But despite several tries, she had

remained firm on not letting Mishti wear a sari. It was very, very annoying.

When everyone had left, Mishti stayed back and helped Dida neatly fold and put away the remaining saris back in their place.

'Tultul doesn't know what a gem she has.' Dida patted the little girl.

'She doesn't think I'm such a gem!'

'I'm sure she does.'

'Then why she won't let the gem wear a sari on Chumki-di's wedding day?' Mishti pouted. 'I'm sure she will fuss when you dress me in that murgi of yours. I don't like that!'

'Muga not murgi, child! Mishti, have you ever asked your mother why she won't let you wear a sari? It isn't such a big deal after all?'

'That's what I keep telling her. It is not a big deal at all!'

Dida suddenly became serious. 'You do know that your Ma's front two teeth are false?'

'What?'

And then out came the story which Mishti hadn't known. Dida told her what had happened. When Ma was about ten, the same age as Mishti, she had worn a sari to a wedding. Unaccustomed to wearing a sari and heels, she had stumbled on the stairs. It had been an awful fall and her front two teeth had been knocked out, and she had fractured her wrist.

'The poor girl fainted with pain and the sight of so much blood,' Dida said sadly. 'I blamed myself for letting her wear a sari, and maybe she blamed herself too.'

SNEAKINESS RUNS IN THE FAMILY

'Maybe it isn't her but her fear which is making her so unreasonable?' Dida said. For the first time, she looks worried rather than excited about Plan B.

Suddenly, fooling her daughter and going behind her back didn't seem like such a good idea to her. God forbid if Mishti too had a mishap! She would have only herself to blame.

Mishti was quiet too. What a terrible thing to happen. She had goosebumps just thinking of all that pain her mother had been in. She also thought if they went through with Plan B, maybe it would make things uncomfortable between Dida and Ma. Though she would wear flat sandals or her sports shoes with the sari, if she fell despite such precautions, Ma would be angry with Dida.

Mishti suddenly came to a solution and jumped down from Dida's bed. 'I'm coming in a minute!'

She returned in a minute, dragging Ma with her into the room.

'Mishti!' Ma was extremely surprised 'What are you doing?'

'Sit, Ma. Why didn't you tell me the reason behind forbidding me from wearing a sari?'

'What?'

'Yes, Tultul,' Dida intervened. 'You could have told her why you were against her wearing a sari...'

'Oh!' Ma subconsciously rubbed at the slight scar on her wrist. 'You did?'

'That must have been so agonizing, Ma,' Mishti enveloped her mother in a big hug and kissed her cheek hard. 'Poor, poor you!'

'Well...' Ma's eyes became wet, but she started laughing. 'That was years ago. Imagine me crying after all those years!'

'I shouldn't have let you wear those heels, Tultul.'

'I would have sneakily worn them, Ma. Even if you hadn't allowed me.'

'Hmmm...' Dida's ears perk up when she hears the word 'sneaky'. Suddenly, she burst out, 'Hahahahaha!'

Ma looked completely bewildered.

Soon, Mishti understood and joined in the laughter. 'Sneakiness runs in the family then, right, Dida?'

'I'd say!' Dida said, finally controlling herself.

'What are you two up to now?' Ma said exasperated.

'Before you say anything, Tultul,' Dida spoke up, 'we were indeed sneakily planning something...' and she told Ma about Plan B.

Ma didn't quite know whether to laugh or to be annoyed with her daughter and her mother.

'...Well, now we have a whole new Plan C for tomorrow, with your approval, of course. And no more sneaking behind anybody's back! I'll dress Mishti in a sari but no heels at all. In fact, I will make sure she doesn't have to climb any stairs at all, OK?' Dida comforted Ma.

Ma could just nod. She could now see how much Mishti wanted to wear a sari. She couldn't let her bad experience affect the little girl's day—she couldn't.

THE WEDDING DAY DAWNS

The wedding day dawns bright and clear, much to the delight of everyone.

Mishti jumps up to the other-worldly sounds of uloo dhwani and races downstairs. She doesn't want to miss anything!

'Uloo dhwani has nothing to do with "ulloos", a.k.a., owls. But this is a rather loud, sometimes bewildering sound perfected by Bengali women as an auspicious sound,' said Ma.

Mishti had been educated, and she was convinced that no evil could stand its ground in front of that sound.

All the women and girls have gathered in the dining hall where Chumki sits on a low stool. Ma and Mami are preparing a large bowl of milk and turmeric paste.

This is a ceremony Mishti is familiar with. She has been to some haldi ceremonies in Jaipur too. She doesn't particularly like the way people smear haldi on each other's faces—quite like Holi, except for the fact that there is turmeric instead of colours. Everyone else, though, seems to be enjoying a lot. Mishti watches from beside the almirah, quite hidden from the view. But not for long. Soon, Runu-di chases after her with a handful of haldi and, before Mishti can escape, she finds her face smeared with the yellow paste.

'Stop, Runu-di, stop!' she shouts.

'This will make you glow tonight at the wedding!'

'No thanks!' and she runs to the safety of their room and to wash off the goop.

'It is a ploy to get everyone to bathe early!' she says to Ma, who's herself half yellow with turmeric and preparing for the bath.

She looks up. 'That really must be how it all started! Good logic, Mishtu!'

The house looks straight out of a fairytale when Mishti goes downstairs after her bath.

Long alternating garlands of bright yellow marigolds and roses hang along walls and intertwined with the railings. A beautiful 'mandap' has been erected in the centre of the large hall. On the four corners there are banana trees and the 'walls' are countless of rajnigandha and roses. It is almost like a shower of fragrant flowers.

'Hello, Neat Cone!' Chumki-di appears, glowing even more than usual and her hair still dripping wet. 'Isn't everything lovely!'

'Luuuvely!' Mishti sighs. 'I'm going to get married at home too!'

'Yes!' Runu-di agrees. 'It is so much nicer than a wedding hall, isn't it?'

It is indeed so. Mishti had been mentally comparing it to another wedding she had attended. This was so much nicer and every member of the family could be a part of everything.

The whole house is fragrant with the aroma of marigolds, roses, and mogra everywhere. The gently curling smoke rising from dhoop made everything feel sacred. Mouthwatering smells waft as streams of delicacies emerge endlessly from the kitchen.

Within no time, evening dawns, and everybody gets busy dressing up because the wedding is in a few hours.

'Come, Mishti,' Ma yells. 'Let us get you ready.'

Mishti follows Ma to her room skipping like a lamb. She feels thrilled and relaxed that there is no need to hide her plan from Ma.

Inside, everyone is busy getting ready. Five didis are crowding around two mirrors, peering at their saris. Unfamiliar as they are to saris, all of them are looking flustered.

'Uff,' Abha-di straightens the pleats yet again. 'Why can't they stay straight? I wish we could have gone in casuals.'

'Nooo,' Mishti frowns. 'This is far, FAAAR prettier!'

'And specialer.'

'I don't think that's a word.'

'It isn't,' Mishti nods. 'But it is perfect!'

Just then the door opens, and everyone stares open-mouthed. Framed just within the door is Elegance herself. Mishti can't take her eyes off Dida. She is wearing a lovely grey and silver sari. Her hair is neatly tied in an elegant bun, and her earlobes carry two tiny silver earrings, which shine like stars. A small pendant hangs around her neck on an almost invisible silver chain. Her dark bindi adds a regal finish. Mishti hopes that she will look half as pretty when she's old as her grandmother.

All the didis crowd around her. 'How do you do it Dida!'

Dida smiles with pleasure. She has always been known for her sense of style.

'This room looks like the green room of my college,' she says, tucking her pallu around her waist. 'Let me help you girls!'

And she runs nimbly from one didi to another, helping one to straighten her sari, clipping the pallu just so for another, and doing up another one's hair in her signature style.

Abha-di too is busy doing everyone's hair and make-up, but, of course, she is a beautician. Tara-di is playing the role of her assistant, handing her clips and other cosmetics. All the didis soon finish draping the beautiful saris. How different they look! How graceful!

'You know, I now think going retro was the best idea.' Tara says. 'Where would we find such gorgeous saris now?'

'I know,' Puploo-di says flourishing her graceful peacock blue silk pallu. 'Now I can see how real style never goes out of fashion.'

'These were sourced from all across India,' Dida says proudly. 'Some are even handprinted!'

'You've kept them in mint condition, Didu!'

'And now they're for you, for keeps.' Dida says. 'You take these traditional saris with you. They'll never go out of fashion, I assure you.'

'Take them?'

'For keeps?'

The girls can't believe their ears. Dida was parting with her saris!

'Are you sure, Dida?' Abha asks 'We will return them in mint condition, just like you said...'

'No,' Dida says firmly. 'They are yours! Seeing you all, looking so lovely and happy, I realize that you girls are giving my saris a second lease of life...' She stops, clears her throat, and continues, 'It is much better than them languishing in my almirahs...'

Mishti edges her way among the didis to reach Dida.

Dida takes her to an almirah and pulls out the sari, but it isn't the one that she had shown Mishti. 'This isn't the muga?' Mishti caresses the silky smooth fabric. She doesn't say anything but this vibrant red, white, and gold Benarasi sari is even prettier than the muga. Mishti hasn't seen this one before—but somehow it looks familiar.

'Are you sure, Dida?'

'Yes,' Dida says briskly. 'Just don't spill anything on it!'

'Oh,' Mishti says fervently 'I'll starve if I have to!'

'Nothing so drastic,' and Dida hands her a beautiful kurti in white and gold brocade. 'But yes, be careful. This one is really special!'

Dida is an expert at draping a perfect sari and, within minutes, the little girl is transformed into a princess in the red and gold sari. She is handed over to Abha-di who braids her thick curls, pins a whole lot of thick mogra gajras, and then applies the tiniest bit of kohl that make Mishti's big eyes even bigger.

Just then they hear a loud knock on the door.

'Mishti, ready?'

The didis, Dida, and Mishti stifle their giggles.

'Mishti?' Ma calls again, impatiently.

'Coming, coming,' Mishti replies and unlatches the door.

Ma's face is a sight! Her eyes become as big as saucers and her jaw drops!

Baba and Dadu are standing behind her, and their reactions are identical. All three are gaping at the adorable princess standing smiling in front of them!

'Oh my God!' Ma gasps faintly, reaching out and slightly

stroking Mishti's cheek to make sure that it was indeed Mishti in front of her.

'My baby girl!' Ma is suddenly dabbing her eyes. 'In *this* sari!' She turns to Dida. 'Ma, you dressed Mishti in my wedding sari!'

'What!' Now it is Mishti's turn to be surprised. Of course, she had seen the sari in the wedding pictures; that's why it looked familiar.

Dida laughs delightedly. 'Isn't she looking as pretty as you had!'

Dadu and Baba step ahead and hug the little girl.

The didis all look at this lovely sight, and their eyes look suspiciously moist.

Mishti can sort of see why. She has often heard her mother say that she's growing up too fast and look sadly at her. She suddenly also understands that this could have been another reason why her mother was insisting that she wear her Cinderella frock. She did not want to see her baby girl looking all grown-up in a sari!

Mishti truly is growing older and wiser, which is why she knows she must do something before everyone becomes too sentimental.

'I know why you all look close to tears,' she says brightly. 'You're afraid I will steal the show!'

Everyone bursts into laughter.

But then the door next to theirs opens, and Chumki-di emerges from her room.

There's no way anyone can steal her thunder.

She's looking regal in red and gold. But of course, she is the BRIDE. It is her day after all.

'Hey, Neat Cone!' she smiles. 'We match!'

They did and how!

'You're both wearing your own mothers' wedding saris,' Dida informs everyone. And immediately there were clamours of other didis asking whether Dida had their mothers' saris, too.

'You're a trendsetter, Ma,' Mishti's mother says. 'Fancy designers won't like you one bit if everyone started wearing their own mothers' wedding saris for their weddings and stopped buying their expensive clothes!'

'And this so beautifully fulfils the four pillars of that old English rhyme,' Dida says. 'Something old, something new, something borrowed, something blue!'

Chumki takes a quick look at her attire. Her sari was old, her ornaments were new, the veil covering her head was borrowed from Mishti's mother, and her ring was sapphire—a deep, deep blue! 'Yes, all fulfilled!' she declares happily.

'What do they symbolize though?' someone asks.

'Old is for continuity,' Ma explains. 'New is for the future, borrowed is for humility and borrowed happiness, and the blue is a symbol of purity.'

'What a lovely idea!' Chumki says emotionally. 'I love the idea of continuity and humility.'

Just then Sumat-da comes along and hands Mishti a big bouquet of red and white roses. 'Come on, ladies,' he says with a theatrical bow. 'Everyone is waiting!'

Mishti, the neat cone, holds the bouquet proudly as she walks Chumki to the mandap.

A beaming Mohit is already there. He is dressed in an off-white dhoti panjabi, looking very much like a hero out of Bengali movies.

The didis take their places around the mandap amidst a lot of teasing and laughter, but then the pandit starts the mantras and everybody falls silent, overcome by the solemnity of the occasion.

Mishti sits down carefully and holds Chumki-di's hands.

'What about the tonnes of money that you're saving?' she whispered, suddenly remembering that Dida had said that was a secret.

Chumki looks at Mohit, and they both smile.

'We will be holding medical and surgical camps over the year for people who cannot afford them...' Mohit says.

'What a super idea!'

'Of course! That's what won my heart.'

So, it's true, Mishti thought, *Mohit is really the kindest person ever.*

Somehow, it is like everything has come a perfect full circle.

GLOSSARY

Jaata: useless/mindless
Malai chingri: prawn cooked in coconut milk
Koraishooti kochuri: kachoris stuffed with a filling of peas
Aloor dom: a Bengali potato-based delicacy
Channar jilipi: jalebis made of cottage cheese (paneer)
Bordi: elder sister
Gaaye holud: an auspicious ceremony where turmeric paste is applied by family members on the bridal couple on the day of the wedding and is followed by a ceremonial bath.
Bou-bhaat: The first meal prepared by the new bride at her husband's house
Shubho Drishti: auspicious first sight of the groom and the bride on the wedding day
Biye Baari: a house (baari) where a wedding (biye) is taking place
Payesh: a popular dessert made of milk and rice especially made on auspicious occasions
Aiburo Bhaat: the last meal the bride and groom have as bachelors
Tatto: special gifts of new clothes and sweets for the bride and groom and their families, that are exchanged just before the wedding day
Aloo Sabji: potatoes cooked in a gravy
Natni: granddaughter
Khunti: the spatula used for cooking
Shukto: a light preparation of vegetables
Bhaja moog daal: lentils made of dry-roasted pulses
Aloo and begun bhaja: fried potatoes and fried eggplant
Kosha mangsho: well-cooked mutton curry
Luchi and aloo dom: puris accompanied with white potatoes cooked in a special gravy
Dekhachchi toke: 'I'll show you!'

Godavari Days

Sarabjeet Garcha

A NOTE BY THE AUTHOR

Growing up in a city steeped in myth, I often felt as if I were living in a dream. The river Godavari made the dream richer. Its banks, relatively free of concrete in the 1980s and '90s, were as accessible to us children as they were to adults. The building I lived in stood on its left bank. It was not unusual to come by swimmers who plunged into its waters without any fear of catching skin disease. I wouldn't say that the river was totally free of pollution, but it looked and felt clean.

Five trees grew right in front of my house: a peepal, a vilayati imli, a jujube, a cluster fig, and a keekar. The vilayati imli tree was in the peepal's tight hug. They looked inseparable. Every Saturday evening, my grandmother lit a diya at the foot of the peepal. Every few months, a goatherd equipped with a sickle climbed the tree to prune its spreading branches. His herd loved peepal leaves. The tree still stands, but the building near it has been pulled down. The keekar and the jujube are there, too.

As a child, I celebrated Ganesh Chaturthi with great enthusiasm. To the best of my knowledge, ours was not the only Sikh family to rejoice in the ten-day festivities. We, too, set up a Ganesh idol in our house. On the tenth day, my friends and I, walking barefoot, carried the idol to Ram Kund for immersion.

Over the past forty years, Nasik has transformed from a sleepy town to a bustling city, but it still has its quiet pockets. Although I have fictionalized real locations in the city, this story is essentially a work of the imagination.

The water filtration technology mentioned in the story is based on the use of protein nanofibrils, an emerging field in nanoscience. The Tukaram poem quoted by the usal woman is from Dilip Chitre's *Says Tuka.*

THE RIVER AND THE MOUNTAIN

Gazing out of his bedroom window, Tushar takes in the view of the river in the mellowing afternoon. His nose detects a hint of mustiness in the air, but in his mind's eye, he sees the waters sparkling and the banks lush with flowering trees. He believes that his bare feet feel cool

on the floor because of his kinship with the river. It's as if the Godavari's gentle waves are lapping over his toes and ankles, a swift breeze caressing them, a cool blooming on his skin. The sky is birdless. It's as if all the birds have decided to sleep in the depths of the blue above.

Face pressed against the horizontal bars of the grille, he scans the slow curve of the water's course. If he lived on the opposite side of the river, the world would have seemed so different—and the river, shorter. But he feels lucky to be living on the Godavari's left bank because his window on the ninth floor offers him a wider view.

On the right, he sees the river flowing past a cluster of trees behind a low bridge. On the left, he sees it flow to the Ahilyabai Holkar Bridge. Built by the British when they ruled India, it was earlier called Victoria Bridge. The river runs over a small dam under the bridge and drops into Gandhi Talaav, a D-shaped pool. From above, the talaav looks calm.

The small tributary of the river enters a narrow canal from under the bridge, running parallel to the straight edge of Gandhi Talaav. Then, it meets a square pool called Lakshman Kund. A tiny bridge separates it from a bigger pool called Ram Kund. This is the city's main bathing ghat, bringing together pilgrims and devotees from all over.

Ram Kund also marks the turn of the river towards the south. That is why the Godavari is also called Dakshin Vahini.

Tushar has never taken a dip in the river.

'It is too polluted to bathe in,' says Baba. The thick mats of water hyacinth on the water prove him right. But beneath the Godavari, which has become an unhealthy shade of green,

Tushar sees another river—spotless, odourless, safe enough to swim in. He wants this hidden river to emerge in its full glory.

Thanks to Miss Shirley Vaz, his English teacher, he learnt a new word at school today: *revere*. Before he made this word his own, he used to love the river, but now he knows exactly what he feels about it. *I revere the river*, he says to himself, convinced that the Godavari can hear him.

This reverence began five years ago when Tushar was just six years old. He still remembers his first conversation with Baba about it:

'Where does the river come from, Baba?'

'From a mountain, son. The Brahmagiri.'

'Where is it?'

'In Trimbakeshwar, a town 32 kilometres away from where we live.'

Tushar repeated the name, feeling the slow bristle of the first syllable on his tongue. He saw the mountain when he closed his eyes. It was covered with trees. He couldn't see the river, but his ears were suddenly filled with the music of the birds in the trees.

FRIENDS FOREVER

Right next to Tushar's building is a sanatorium. A cobblestone path runs between its eight identical cottages, tucked among mango, guava, jamun, chikoo, and frangipani trees. The tiled roofs, whitewashed walls, and blue-and-white doors of the cottages look bright against the various shades of green all around. Large windows allow ample natural light into the interiors. The steps leading to the veranda of each cottage are flanked by jasmine shrubs.

Most of the sanatorium's ground runs level before lowering into a slope that meets the riverbank. A towering neem tree stands majestically at the head of this incline. Tushar can see its vast canopy from his living room window.

The neem tree makes Tushar think of the Brahmagiri. Whenever he wishes to touch the mountain, he simply touches the tree instead. 'Wood is the softer cousin of stone,' his mother had once said. He feels he is a brother to both.

He owed this special feeling to Miss Shirley Vaz, who is a keen storyteller. The tales she tells paint vivid pictures. Her soothing voice makes not only the characters come alive but also the trees that surround them. The trees in her stories seem as real as the neem tree and play vital roles in the lives of their human companions.

Even though it is Saturday, Tushar is up early. But no school doesn't mean no work. In fact, it means extra work, even special work—something he can't afford to miss.

'Aai, when shall we go to Bhaji Bazaar?' he asks his mother.

'Soon, bala,' says Aai. 'Let me finish cooking first.'

'What's for breakfast?'

'Misal pav.'

'Wow!' Tushar exclaims, bouncing up and down. He can already smell the spicy curry simmering in the kitchen.

'Don't do that,' warns Aai. 'The folks downstairs might be tapping their toes to a different rhythm.'

'But that's no reason to stop our own music,' Tushar protests.

Aai doesn't fail to notice a mischievous glint in his eye, and he too gets the clue from her gaze. He knows better than to invite Aai's anger, so he stops.

'Aai,' he says, 'can I ask Sukhbir to join us for breakfast?'

'Why not?' Aai smiles. 'You know I love his questions about Marathi food.'

Tushar makes

to go out, but Aai stops him. 'Wait, bala,' she says. 'I can WhatsApp his mom.'

'I won't be long, Aai.'

Tushar rarely misses an opportunity to go downstairs.

Sukhbir, a Sikh boy Tushar's age, lives in an old building beside the sanatorium. He loves all things Maharashtrian. Half of the property where Sukhbir's building stands belongs to a garage, which operates from a shed close to the main road. The open space between the shed and the building is used as a truckyard. When there are no trucks, children from the neighbourhood use it as a playground.

About 15 feet in front of the building, a few trees, shrubs, and bushes form a sparse but green screen. It partly hides the four ground-floor entrances from the truckyard. The very first door on the left is Sukhbir's.

Tushar doesn't need to knock, as the doors in this building remain open all day. Thinking of catching Sukhbir by surprise, he approaches stealthily. Sukhbir is engrossed in combing his waist-length hair, his head bent. Each stroke begins at the nape of his neck, glides up to the crown, and then moves to the tapering edge of the slow, black cascade of hair. After repeating this ritual a few times, he gathers his hair, twists it like a rope, and then coils it into a knot on top of his head. Finally, he places a white handkerchief over the topknot and secures it with a rubber band.

Some boys in the neighbourhood used to make fun of Sukhbir's topknot. One day, when Sukhbir was on his way back from school, someone shouted, '*Haath mein kada, oopar dahi vada!*'

Sukhbir ignored the jibe and continued walking. Tushar, who was nearby, heard everything.

'Yes!' Tushar yelled back, looking the bully straight in the eye. It was Munna. 'He *has* a kada on his hand. And if he wants, he can smash your teeth with it. How would you like that?'

Munna became silent.

'As for the dahi vada,' Tushar went on, 'it's a rare gift. If you don't know its value, just keep your mouth shut.'

From that day on, nobody dared mock Sukhbir.

They have become best friends ever since.

Catching sight of Tushar standing at the door, Sukhbir's eyes light up.

'Is my fine sardar friend finally ready?' says Tushar. 'Why don't you start tying a turban?'

Sukhbir smiles. 'Arrey, just fixing my jooda takes me at least fifteen minutes. A full-fledged turban would take much longer,' he says.

'Of course. A fault-finder like you can take forever! Now, how about a hearty breakfast after all this hard work?'

'I'm in!'

Right away, both of them break into a run. In less than a minute, they arrive at the elevator shaft of Tushar's building. Instead of pressing the button, they look at each other, smile, and rush to the staircase.

When they reach the landing between the fifth and the sixth floor, both begin to pant.

'It's the continuous laughter that is making us huff and puff,' says Tushar.

'Six is nothing,' says Sukhbir. 'I can easily climb another twenty floors without a break.'

'Why just twenty? I'm sure you'll take the stairs even in the Burj Khalifa and reach the top floor without having to stop.'

At this, they burst into another bout of laughter.

THIRST

Stepping out of the main gate of their complex, Tushar and Aai turn right and arrive at a three-point crossing. A bust of Shivaji stands atop a traffic island. Three arms of this crossroads are level, but the fourth is a short but steep slope lined with shops. Tushar delights in walking down this slope. The potter's shop on the left is his favourite. Walking by, he always slows down to take a closer look at the earthen pots, clay lamps, surahis, piggy banks, flowerpots, roof tiles, and figures of gods and goddesses.

The road splits near the base of the slope, marked by a sweet shop with a tiled roof. Tushar and Aai keep to their right, walking down the small path parallel to the river, past the three-storey changing facility at Ram Kund, past the Ardhanarinateshwar and Vishweshwar temples, past Dutondya Maruti, to the spot where the vegetable market starts.

Here, the chatter of vendors dampens the river's murmur, but their fusion still sounds sweet. The bazaar is a criss-cross of makeshift canopies, but not every vendor has one. Some of them sit under a single umbrella fastened to a stick, their faces weathered. Those with no overhead canvas for cover do not seem to mind the February sun too much. Some have low tables with drawers to keep cash and loose change, while others tuck their money under tarpaulin sheets on which they sit cross-legged. Some call out loud to customers, while others wait in silence.

Hillocks of dry chillies look as inviting as mounds of potatoes, onions, and tomatoes. There's okra, aubergine, bitter gourd, drumstick, shepu, spinach, cucumber, cabbage, cauliflower, peas, beans, bottle gourd, and sponge gourd.

'Look, Aai,' says Tushar, pointing to a woman sitting behind two large and several small wicker baskets. It's the woman who sells usal. Whether Aai buys anything else from the market or not, purchasing usal is a must whenever she is with Tushar.

'I know,' she says, and they both walk towards the woman.

'How are you, Kaku?' Aai asks the woman.

'All is well by Vitthal's grace, daughter,' says the woman, smiling.

She doesn't ask how much usal she should weigh. She knows because Aai is a regular customer. As usual, she starts by scooping a few handfuls of matki sprouts from the biggest basket, followed by two or three handfuls of moong sprouts. Putting the sprouts on one plate of the weighing scale,

she picks some chana, chawli, peas, and chickpeas from the small baskets and drops them on the sprouts. Then, she lifts the scale, weighs the usal, and tilts the plate over a newspaper. Carefully wrapping it, she secures the parcel with a cotton thread.

When Aai hands her the money, the woman fishes out some change from a cloth purse tucked in the waist fold of her sari. It's a patchwork quilt of a purse—rectangular, with three pockets sewn along its length. Tushar feels as if each pocket preserves the blessings of the Tridev—the top, Brahma's; the middle, Vishnu's; the bottom, Shiva's. So, when she gives Aai the balance, she appears to be sharing some of the grace that the gods have sent her way.

Maybe that is why she doesn't have a QR code to accept digital payments, Tushar says to himself. She doesn't even own a mobile phone. Once, when Aai asked her why, she said, 'I hear Vitthal already. The mobile's chatter wouldn't muffle his voice, but it could distract me. I am happy without all the noise.'

Then, after a pause, she quoted an abhang:

I was so thirsty
I drank up my thirst
I was so hungry
I ate my hunger

My very self
Became nothing
Vitthal
Found me clean

There was no room
For desire
The mind collapsed
At his feet

What remained
Was still Tuka
His life was lost
To itself

Tushar wasn't sure that he understood everything the woman said, but that didn't stop him from listening. He didn't remember the entire abhang, but he couldn't forget the first two lines. Later, he asked Baba about it. Baba recalled it immediately, and told him what it meant: if you really want something with all your heart, you forget that you want it in the end. Forgetting helps you achieve because it purifies desire. And when desire is pure, action is clean.

It all sounded like a lovely riddle. 'But Baba,' asked Tushar, 'why didn't Tukaram say so directly?'

Tushar will never forget the smile that lit up Baba's face. 'Because what is direct is not always beautiful.'

The word *thirsty* in the very first verse of the abhang brings him back to the river. When he looks around, his heart sinks. The riverbed is covered in concrete. He tries hard to locate the kunds, or pools, that Baba often talks about. Didn't he say there were seventeen kunds? Yes, he did. But except for Lakshman Kund and Ram Kund, he can't make out any of the others. He recalls some of the names, though: Dhanush

Kund, Sita Kund, Dutondya Maruti Kund, Surya Kund, and Khandoba Kund.

'Aai,' he says.

'Yes, bala?' Aai can sense that something is bothering him.

'Why did they cover the riverbed with concrete?'

'It was done a long time ago for a development project during the Kumbh Mela.'

'But Aai, why make the river look like a canal?'

'These ghats were built more than 300 years ago. Perhaps they wanted to give them a modern look.'

'Do you like it?'

'I don't. I can't. The kunds paved in stone had a charm that concrete cannot match. And all this concrete is blocking the natural flow of the Godavari.'

'How?'

'There were many natural springs in the riverbed. They helped replenish the river even during dry periods.'

The mention of underground springs reminds him of a well behind Sukhbir's building. Decades ago, people stopped drawing water from it because it tasted bad. When the river is in flood, the water level in the well rises. It is as if the river does not want the well to dry up, even if nobody drinks its water.

Suddenly, Tushar feels very thirsty. He pictures a glass of water floating towards him and disappearing just when its rim is about to touch his lips.

Does the Godavari also feel parched?

He now stands on the lowest step of the ghat near the vegetable market. He unscrews his water bottle, pours water into the cap, and empties it slowly into the river. He fills the cap again—this time for himself.

WHEN IT POURS IN NASIK

Monsoons in Nasik are rarely late. Baba believes that the official date for the arrival of the rains in the ancient city is 7 June, give or take a week. So long as they come, nobody bothers about their punctuality. One cannot, of course, expect clouds to plan their visits according to weather forecasts.

When it pours in Nasik, even Tushar's dreams become rain-soaked, letting out the same scent that rises from dry soil after the season's first shower. Within days, the city transforms into a breathtakingly beautiful landscape.

Tushar has heard about the magic carpet, but it is nothing compared to the one that covers his neighbourhood. Every road branching out of the city leads to lush beauty. Tushar need not travel too far to seek it. A 10-kilometre drive with Baba in any direction is enough to land him in the heart of nature's bounty.

The road to Trimbakeshwar is his favourite. After the rains, it is lined with small and large waterfalls, each outshining the other. No weekend seems well spent without a visit to Trimbakeshwar. The queues outside the Shiva temple are too long to deal with, but a mere look at the Brahmagiri counts as a full darshan. With its saddle-shaped top shrouded with swirling mist, the mountain beckons Tushar. Several streams roll down its slope. It also has a waterfall that appears to be cascading upwards because of strong winds.

Tushar and Sukhbir become quite adventurous in this season. Both take special interest in sticky bristlegrass, which is to be found only during monsoon.

It's bristlegrass day today. Having plucked a few tufts of the light green grass, they are waiting patiently. After half an hour, they see Babbu coming towards them. Tushar elbows Sukhbir and stealthily passes his panicles to him. To hide the grass missiles, Sukhbir crosses his arms behind his back.

Babbu is a bit of a bully, but he became friends with Tushar and Sukhbir when he realized that he cannot intimidate them.

'Hey, Sukkhi and Tushar,' says Babbu, 'let's play dabba ispies.'

They notice that Babbu is already carrying a tin can for the game.

'But Babbu,' says Tushar, 'dabba ispies between just the three of us won't be much fun. We need at least five more playmates to make it interesting.'

Seeing that Tushar has caught Babbu's attention, Sukhbir says, 'Give me two minutes to have a glass of water. I'll be right back.'

Luckily, to go home, Sukhbir must face the other direction as Babbu. After taking a few steps, Sukhbir stops, turns, and flings a tuft of burr bristlegrass at Babbu's back. His aim is perfect. The tuft sticks to Babbu's T-shirt.

Although Tushar saw what happened, his face didn't show it. Babbu doesn't notice a thing. He is busy talking.

'Well,' says Babbu. 'Let me see if Sonal, Sunaina, Prashant, Pinty, and Rajbir can join us.'

Sonal and Sunaina are sisters, Prashant is Pinty's older brother, and Rajbir is Sukhbir's younger brother. Babbu usually prefers to follow the diktats of his selfishness and stay blissfully unaware of others' existence. But when it's time for team games, his memory shows a great capacity for recall.

'I don't think they'll come,' he goes on. 'Our exams are only a fortnight away. So, all of us should have our noses buried in books.'

Nobody has seen Babbu with a book. It's a wonder that he even passed his exams. Not that his grades are anything to be proud of, but he loves to offer advice.

By the time Sukhbir is back, Babbu begins to scratch his back. The burr dislodges and falls off.

'What's wrong?' says Sukhbir, feigning surprise.

'Don't know, yaar,' says Babbu, still scratching. 'I think an ant has bitten me.'

'Come on, Babbu,' says Tushar. 'You are too thick-skinned for ants.'

By now, the two accomplices can hardly control themselves. As soon as they burst out laughing, Babbu realizes that he has been tricked. Turning over, he sees the telltale burr on the ground and pretends to act normal, but his eyes reflect his anger.

The three boys are standing near the barbed-wire fence that marks the boundary between the sanatorium and Sukhbir's building. Thickets of lantana and undershrub have added to the width of the fence.

Babbu points to a jewel bug hovering over a lantana flower. Thanks to this little insect, his anger seems to have dissipated. He gingerly draws closer to the bug. It looks beautiful with black dots on its brilliant green outer shell. As soon as it settles on a leaf, Babbu captures it with a swoop of his hand. Fishing out a perforated matchbox from his pocket, he opens his palm and gently presses the bug with the ring finger of his left hand. The matchbox is balanced between the other three fingers and the base of his palm.

'Tushar, open the matchbox for me,' Babbu says.

'Let it go,' Tushar insists.

'I will, but only if you help me with the matchbox.'

'As you wish.'

Tushar takes the matchbox from Babbu and pulls it open. Babbu lets go of the bug, puts it into the matchbox, and slides it shut.

'Want to see a new kind of kite?' he asks.

'Like what?' says Sukhbir.

'Wait and watch,' Babbu says, this time pulling out a cotton string from his pocket.

'Do you always carry these things?' Tushar is curious.

'It pays to be well-equipped, especially during this season,' says Babbu.

He makes a noose at one end of the string and asks Tushar to open the matchbox. 'Just a bit,' he advises.

Tushar does as he is told, not because he likes doing it, but because he wants to set the bug free. Babbu pinches it between the thumb and index finger of his left hand, making sure not to squeeze too hard. Then, sliding one of its legs into the noose, he tightens the knot and releases the bug. Buzzing, it tries to fly away, but can only lift itself as far as the length of the string.

'You like the paperless kite?' Babbu says.

'You are cruel, Babbu!' Tushar protests.

'Set it free,' says Sukhbir. 'You'll pull its leg off!'

'Mind your own business, nature lovers.' Babbu doesn't seem to be in the mood to listen.

Just then, Babbu's mother comes looking for him. The sight of her approaching fills him with terror. He tries to imagine what colour his cheeks will be when she gives him her special left-hand treatment. His grip on the string slackens, and he lets go of the jewel bug. But before it flies away, Tushar grabs the string and says, 'Sukkhi, go get a pair of scissors.'

Sukhbir can already foresee what Tushar will do. It doesn't take him more than a minute to be back with the thing asked for.

Tushar pulls the string towards himself as lightly as he can. The bug is still trying to break free. He holds it between his thumb and index finger. Taking the scissors close to the bound leg of the insect, he cautiously cuts the string.

Tushar and Sukhbir are thrilled to see the stunning jewel bug fly away.

WHAT THEY SAW

Raju Katkar works at Baba's sawmill. He belongs to the Katkari tribe, known for its ancient connection to forests. Eighteen years ago, Baba rescued him from a brick kiln. In fact, his parents handed him over to Baba so he could get a better life. He was only seven years old then. Now, the sawmill is both his home and workplace.

Baba taught Raju to read and write and sent him to school. Baba wanted him to live with his family. He did, but only for a couple of years. Later, when he started accompanying Baba to the mill, he liked it so much that he wanted to be there all the time.

After he completed high school, Raju said he did not want to study further.

'Are you sure?' Baba asked.

'Yes,' said Raju.

'Think it over again.'

'I have made up my mind, Baba.' Like Tushar, Raju also calls him Baba.

'What will you do?'

'Help you at the mill.'

Now, the *shiooo shiooo shiooo* of the bandsaw is music to his ears and the smell of fresh sawdust is fragrance to his nose.

He lives in a two-room log cabin.

Every four months, Raju goes to Thane to see his parents.

Tushar is at the mill today. He loves talking to Raju, who is fourteen years older than him. Raju always talks about trees—their beauty, silence, unity; their resilience, patience, benevolence; their secrets.

'Raju Dada,' says Tushar, 'Baba and you call yourselves nature worshippers, yet you cut down trees. How can lumberjacks like you be tree lovers?'

'Tushar,' Raju says, his voice calm as ever, 'the truth is much deeper than what you see on the surface.'

'Meaning?'

'I never fell trees protected by the Forest Department. Baba and I respect the law. But because we deal in timber, we have to get it from somewhere.'

'So, where do you get it from?'

'From the trees on private property. We don't need felling permission for some species, like eucalyptus, babul, subabul, drumstick, false ashoka, rubberwood, lac, and poplar.'

'Why so?'

'Take subabul, for example. It is not a species native to India. It not only grows fast but also produces seed pods by the thousands. The wind spreads the seeds far and wide. So do birds and animals.'

'Is that bad?'

'Not bad, really. But too many subabul trees easily eat up the space where native species can flourish.'

'I see.'

'Besides, subabul bark and pulp are used to make paper. So is eucalyptus. Thanks to their rapid growth, these trees have shown no signs of depletion so far.'

Tushar knows that Raju owes his love for trees as much to Baba as to his biological parents. Baba runs the last of the two or three sawmills in the city. Others have been shut down.

Twenty-four years ago, the entire mill burned down because of a short circuit. All timber turned into charcoal. Aajoba used to run it then. The calamity struck on a windy summer night. Baba was to appear for the last paper of his final-year BCom exams, but when he got the news, he chose to go to the mill instead. He didn't set foot in college after that.

The mill was only partially insured. So, the compensation Aajoba received did not cover even a twentieth of the loss. He managed to sell the charcoal to a company that made black toothpowder, but the money from the sale was too little to cause hope for the future. Baba, however, decided to take matters into his own hands. Standing by Aajoba like a pillar, he didn't look back.

Baba took the fire at the sawmill as a sign of nature's wrath. He realized that if he didn't take the cue, he would ultimately have to pay for it. That is when he became curious about trees and fell in love with them. But then, he did not simply sit and think about trees, but started planting them.

He also maintains a regular supply of seeds at the mill so that every customer receives not only timber but also a handful of seeds. However, he does not share his passion for trees on social media.

'If you truly love trees and learn their ways,' he says, 'you won't care for false fame. The real world is much more than a storm of "likes".'

On slow afternoons, father, son, and foster son exchange stories—and sometimes, there is just silence.

One day, the conversation veers to tamarind.

Baba says that the imli from Nasik is of the highest quality. No wonder, Aai doesn't find the packed imli sold in malls and shops to be tangy enough. Truth be told, even the ripe kind—no matter where it is from—isn't as tangy as the unripe, knobby tamarind he ate as a schoolboy.

He used to buy it from a woman sitting cross-legged outside the school gate, a cloth spread in front of her on the dirt road, small knolls of imli pods set in neat rows on a cloth. You would get half a hillock for 25 paise with a complimentary pinch of salt mixed with red chilli powder. She also sold roasted tamarind seeds.

Those days, the roads in the city were lined with tamarind, banyan, and peepal trees, especially the Mumbai–Agra Highway. It was a time when you could easily believe that

Tapovan was a forest in the city, the Forest of Austerities. You knew that the trees on the highways were not any different from those that lived millennia ago.

'Is it true that evil spirits live in tamarind trees?' Tushar asks.

'Well,' Baba says. 'That's a creative way to warn people to keep away from an imli tree. It releases vapours that are believed to be toxic.'

'Do you know why it is called tamarind?' Raju asks. He makes good use of the books he borrows from the public library on Tilak Path.

'I don't.'

'It came to India from Central Africa. Its English name is derived from the Persian word "Tamar-i-Hind", which literally means the "date fruit of India".'

'That's interesting.'

Then, Raju shares a legend related to this tree.

During their exile, Ram, Sita, and Lakshman roamed the Dandakaranya forest. One night, when a terrible storm raged, they took shelter under a tamarind tree. Torrential rain lashed against the tree's dense canopy, but could not touch the trio.

When Ram awoke in the morning, he felt bad about their new-found comfort. As sanyasis, they had vowed to live without refuge. Waking Lakshman, he said that they should move out into the open, although it was still raining.

Then he tried to wake Sita, but she continued sleeping soundly. She looked serene in her sleep. Several days of walking had worn her out. Ram looked at Lakshman for help. Lakshman nodded, and shot an arrow through the canopy. The arrow split the tamarind leaves, and soon, rain and morning light came pouring through. From then on, tamarind leaves have remained small and split.

'Was Nasik part of the Dandakaranya forest?' Tushar asks.

'Yes,' Baba says. 'We Maharashtrians believe that the northern part of the Deccan used to be the Dandakaranya.'

'And our neighbourhood, Panchvati?'

'It's a compound of *panch* and *vati*, which translates to five banyans. Ram, Sita, and Lakshman are believed to have spent some years of their exile in a hut under those five enormous trees. Those banyan trees no longer exist, but their descendants do.'

Tushar can listen to Baba and Raju for hours on end. They ask him to listen to the trees. But Tushar says that when he is with them, he already feels as if he is listening to trees.

THE PROFESSOR

Whenever Tushar needs to be alone, he goes to the sanatorium. The manager, a close friend of Baba's, has allowed him that privilege. The worn cement bench under the massive neem tree is Tushar's favourite spot.

The bench faces the river. As soon as Tushar enters the sanatorium, he notices the back of a white-haired head over the backrest. He pauses, unsure if he should go further. But the early-evening air is so crisp that he can't go back without filling up his lungs with it.

So, he moves on, although his feet don't feel as brisk as they should on a day like this. Walking past the bench, he stands at the top of the slope leading down to the river. A little before the slope becomes level near the riverbank, a barbed-wire fence marks the sanatorium's rear boundary. It is reinforced with nettles and wild bushes.

'Hello.' Tushar hears a voice from behind his back. He turns over and says hello.

A lean man with a pleasant face is seated on the bench. He has on a white dhoti and kurta and a black coat with the buttons undone. His hair, neatly parted on the side, is white, except for a few strands of black.

'Don't let the hair trick you into guessing my age,' says the man. 'It's the dye that left it white. By the time I became aware of the damage, it was already too late.'

Tushar notices a pair of grey eyes behind rimless glasses.

If the man didn't mention it, Tushar wouldn't have noticed the hair at all. 'My friend Sukhbir says that Sikh men don't worry about their hair turning grey.'

'Indeed,' the man agrees. 'I'm sure they also don't bother about going bald. The turban does have other benefits besides making one look impressive.'

Tushar smiles.

'I am Professor Anant Joshi,' says the man, 'a retired biotechnologist.'

'I am Tushar, a sixth-grade student. What brings you here, Professor Joshi?'

'I am recovering from hip replacement surgery.'

'Sorry to hear that.'

'Sorry to hear about the recovery or the surgery?'

'The surgery, of course.' Tushar giggles. Professor Joshi joins in the laughter.

'Can I ask you something?' says Tushar.

'Go on,' says Professor Joshi.

'Can biotechnology help purify water?'

'Of course, it can. It *does*. In fact, that has been the focus of my research in the last two decades.'

'That's amazing!' Tushar is visibly excited. 'Is there a river or a lake that you've been working on?'

'No. But I've been conducting experiments in a lab setting. I've had some promising results, though.'

'Have you thought about applying your research to a local water body?'

'I have, but it's a complex process. It requires collaboration with local authorities, environmental organizations, and communities. And of course, funding.'

'This great river is heavily polluted,' says Tushar, pointing to the Godavari.

'I know, and I feel bad for it. But you and I cannot clean it up alone.'

'Can't we do anything about it?'

'We can. The first step is to create awareness. Eighty per cent of the pollution comes from inside our homes, so we can't keep blaming industries.'

'And what about the thick layer of concrete at Ram Kund?'

'A priest has already been working on getting it removed.'

'Do you know him?'

'I do. He is a good friend. Our goal is the same.'

'Can we join him?'

'Of course. To save the river, we should do everything we can.'

'I want to see him.'

'You will. Soon.'

GANESHA LISTENS

'Is that enough?' asks Sukhbir, dropping a big blob of clay into a mid-size steel bucket Tushar is holding.

'A little more,' says Tushar.

It's the day before Ganesh Chaturthi. They are at the riverbank to get clay to make a Ganesha idol. A flight of stairs behind Sukhbir's building leads down to the river. The sanatorium and Tushar's building do not offer this luxury.

They have resolved not to buy idols made of plaster of Paris this time. Clay, they've been told, is biodegradable.

When the bucket is three-quarters full, Tushar raises a hand, signalling Sukhbir to stop. Squatting on the concrete slab on the water's edge, Sukhbir dips his hands into the river. The submerged fingers squirt slow brown clouds.

'Tushar,' says Sukhbir, 'what was the Marathi word you used a couple of days ago for this side of the river?'

'*Alyaad*,' Tushar replies.

'And *palyaad* means that side?'

'Indeed.'

'What is *alyaad* in English?'

'The near bank, or this side of the river.'

'Near bank? But that's two words.'

'Yes. Miss Vaz confirmed that English does not have a one-word equivalent for either *alyaad* or *palyaad*.'

'Amazing!'

'That's why Baba says that one language is good enough, but *never* enough. So, it's a good idea to learn more than one.'

'Now I know why Papa-ji keeps pushing me to learn Gurmukhi,' says Sukhbir. 'He says that speaking Punjabi at home is one thing but reading it is quite another, and that I can't fully experience my mother language unless I also read it.'

'Listen to your papa-ji. He is right.'

'I will. For now, let's swim over to *palyaad*.'

'No, Sukkhi. Our skin is too delicate for this water.'

'The pollution. I know.'

'Not just that. The current may be difficult for us to navigate. Let the monsoon pass, and let the river become pure again. We'll do it then.'

'But how will it become pure till we have aware citizens like this one?' Sukhbir points to a man standing some distance upstream from where they are.

The man is brushing his teeth vigorously, his feet ankle-deep in water. He seems to be in a hurry, judging by the strokes of his toothbrush. He spits out the toothpaste froth into the river. Then, bending over, he dips his toothbrush, shakes it, runs his thumb on the bristles, and pockets it. Cupping a handful of water, he swishes it around his mouth. The swishing goes on for a while, now the left cheek bulging, now the right. When done, he lets out a forceful squirt. The white jet pierces the river's folds.

Tushar half expects the man to lie face down at the bank, suck water directly from the river without using his hands, and let out a sparkling stream into the waves. Several months ago, he saw a handsome dacoit with a black tilak and black turban do that in a movie.

The man must have come from the two-storey building behind him. It is a chawl with a ridged roof of clay tiles. Situated a few feet away from the river, its right side runs parallel to the water's course.

His afternoon business done, the man turns, walks towards the slope leading to the chawl, and disappears.

'Good that you washed your hands before that white honey could reach here,' says Tushar.

'Yikes!' Sukhbir shakes his head. 'But I'm sure he is not the only bee using the river as a honeycomb.'

'By the way, do you know the story of that bridge?' Tushar points to the right.

'I just know that it has no name. Does it have a story?'

'It does. Baba says it was built in front of his eyes. He was our age then. One afternoon, he and his friends went to the site of the bridge. They were curious as to how a bridge is built.'

'Did they find out how?'

'I'm not sure if they did. An old passerby chased them away. That evening, when Baba got a good dressing down from Aajoba, he guessed that the old man must have known Aajoba. Baba was taken aback to see Aajoba fly into a rage over a small matter. But later, he came to know why.'

'Why?'

'They say that the builders of the bridge sacrifice humans to keep the structure stable.'

'Really?'

'So they say. And children are easy prey.'

'How do they do it?'

'They bury the victim alive in the riverbed or wall them up in one of the pillars. News of this evil ritual spread in the city at the speed of light, and no child was seen near the bridge until it was completed. Thankfully, nobody was reported missing while the construction went on.'

Mouth agape, Sukhbir stares at Tushar.

'Never mind,' says Tushar. 'Let's get going. We've lots to do for Ganesh Chaturthi.'

They climb the stairs, take a left, pass through a small spiked gate, and then turn right. They are now at the base of the ramp near Sukhbir's building. On the left-hand side of this ramp is the sanatorium's fence, running up to the main road.

As they start moving up the slope, a crow appears out of nowhere, swoops down on Sukhbir's head, pecks it with its beak, and flies away as swiftly as it came.

'Watch out!' cries Tushar, who is a few steps behind Sukhbir. But the warning came too late.

Sukhbir feels the handkerchief covering his topknot, then gently frees it from the rubber band's grip. He holds it from two corners. There's an irregular hole in the centre.

'My topknot saved me,' says Sukhbir. 'It could have been my scalp instead of the handkerchief.'

'Thank God!'

'But what made it attack me?'

'Crows become aggressive when they are trying to have babies. Looks like they are nesting in one of the trees around. I think it's the huge neem tree in the sanatorium. So, anyone walking close by seems like a threat to them.'

'I don't think we are that close to wherever they have their nests. And I don't think I am a threat to anyone.'

'You aren't, Sukkhi. But we'll need to learn crow language to tell them that!'

Two hours later, they visit the sawmill. Baba smiles when he sees them enter the gate.

'Raju,' says Baba. 'Get me the bag.'

Raju brings a canvas bag filled with sawdust.

'See if it's too heavy for you,' Baba says.

Tushar lifts it. 'No, Baba,' he says. 'I can easily carry it.'

By the time it is evening, Tushar and Sukhbir are through with the Ganapati decoration. They took Aai's help to make the clay idol. Aai used a small knife and a toothpick to give a nice touch to Ganapati's features.

A wide table, pushed against a wall, has been set aside for Ganesha. It is a custom-made table with a boundary wall running over its perimeter.

Tushar carefully empties the sack of sawdust on the table. Then he and Sukhbir pat some dunes into shape. Folding a piece of newspaper, Tushar places it on the sawdust dunes, making sure that it is at the centre. He likes Lord Ganesha to be surrounded by small brown hills.

The next morning, Tushar and Aai put the Ganesha idol on the soft hills. The air in the drawing room smells of fresh jasmine and incense. Aai plucks a red hibiscus from a flowerpot on the balcony.

Aai, Baba, Tushar, Sukhbir, and Raju stand in a half circle in front of the Ganesha idol. Tushar looks up at his elephant face, the large ears, the pot belly, the broken tusk, and the welcoming trunk curved to the left.

Aai is dressed in a bright blue Paithani sari. Her bangles clink softly as she places a tray of flowers, sweets, and a coconut. Early in the morning, she ordered fresh modak from the famous sweetshop at Ram Kund.

Then comes the aarti. The air grows still for a moment, followed by the sound of clanging cymbals and the ringing of a handbell. The sweet scent of sandalwood smoke curls through the air as everybody joins in the singing. Tushar feels the vibrations in his chest as he chants. His hands are folded in prayer. His heart swells with joy.

After the prayer, they all take turns placing marigold garlands around Ganesha's neck. Aai hands Tushar the hibiscus, and he places it at the idol's feet, whispering his wish. He knows Ganesha will listen—he always does.

ALL FOR THE RIVER

He is out with the professor for the first time. The September morning is crisp, fresh, and fragrant. It is 5.30 a.m., and the streetlights are still on. Those moving about must be either people going to bathe at the river or offer their prayers at the temple, both eager to finish their business before sunrise.

Tushar and the professor stand at the foot of the temple stairs. The pillared entrance balances a small yellow room with three brown windows overhead. Passing by flower sellers and fortune tellers, they climb the stairs and arrive at the platform in front of the Kapaleshwar Temple. The cool stone feels soothing beneath their bare feet. They have left their shoes in the care of a woman selling joss sticks on the first landing below.

This Shiva temple has no Nandi facing the entrance because—as the legend goes—Nandi saved Shiva from sin on this spot and thus became his guru. So the bull doesn't need to be doorkeeper here.

The round clock above the temple door looks out of place. Tushar suddenly becomes aware of the time at his hands, but a quick glance at the clock hands reassures him. It is only 5.40 a.m. Enough time before the school starts.

A middle-aged priest in a burgundy dhoti and pinkish cloth covering his torso steps out of the temple and comes towards them. He shakes hands with Professor Joshi, looks at Tushar, touches him on the shoulder, and says, 'Namaskar, young boy.'

The purohit smells of fresh flowers and incense. Tushar likes his deep voice.

'Here's Vasant Shastri,' says Professor Joshi, patting the priest on the back, 'the purohit who wants to save the Godavari at any cost. He has filed a petition against the city's municipal corporation for blocking the river with concrete.'

'Will all the concrete be removed?' Tushar can't hold back his excitement.

'Ultimately, yes,' says Mr Shastri.

'The petition is showing results,' says Professor Joshi. 'More than 200 tonnes of concrete has already been removed from two spots in the riverbed. As a result, natural springs have started to feed the river again.'

'Amazing!' says Tushar.

'But we have a long way to go,' Mr Shastri says calmly. 'The Godavari is a self-sufficient river. She can look after herself very well if we let her breathe. And she will breathe only when we rid her of all the concrete that was mindlessly poured into her.'

'How can I join you in this movement, Uncle?' asks Tushar.

'By making people care for the river. Whoever loves the Godavari should make an effort to save it.'

'I want to save it.' Tushar clenches his fists.

'Then let's make its gifts and glories known. Let's tell one and all that everybody must protect it.' The purohit is composed as ever. Although he speaks softly, his eyes show that he is determined.

'We are with you, Tushar,' says Professor Joshi.

The early-morning meeting with the purohit leaves Tushar's heart filled with a new sense of purpose. He spends the next few days thinking about ways to make his friends and classmates see what the Godavari has been going through. But he knows he can't just be thinking about it. He must act.

Tushar's first confidante at school is Miss Vaz. With her help, he starts a school club dedicated to the river. They name it Friends of the Godavari. Within days, the club attracts several environment enthusiasts eager to make a difference. Together, they brainstorm ideas to spread awareness about the river's plight. They also hold a poster-making competition and invite students from other schools to take part.

Tushar's excitement makes Baba want to help, too. So, getting over his dislike of social media, he launches an online campaign for the river. Raju and Sukhbir prove to be steadfast supporters. Professor Joshi shares informative posts about the river's history, its ecological importance, and the threats it faces.

It is Sukhbir who gives Tushar a fresh idea for the cause: a prabhat pheri. They design a poster, print 300 copies at home, and go door to door handing them out. When they announce their plan online, slogans come pouring in: 'My River Is Yours Too', 'Let the Godavari Breathe', 'Purity Is Every River's Birthright', 'If You Love It, Leave It', 'It's Our River, Not a Sewer'.

When the day of action comes, Tushar and Sukhbir start sharp at 6 a.m., holding placards. As soon as they exit the apartment complex, they are surprised to find Raju waiting for them outside the gate. Just then, Tushar feels a hand on his shoulder. Turning back, he finds Baba smiling beside Aai.

'Baba! Aai!' Tushar can't say more. His eyes well up.

'Na, my boy,' says Baba. 'It's time to smile.'

'Did you really think we won't join you?' says Aai.

Tushar shakes his head, wiping his tears. Soon, Sonal, Sunaina, Prashant, Pinty, and Rajbir join them, each holding a placard.

Babbu also ambles by. His placard says, 'Our Own River, Not Just Our Past But Also Our Future'.

He winks at Tushar. 'You owe us all a good round of dabba ispies.'

'Of course,' says Tushar.

When they are about to move, a man comes over and asks, 'Can I also join you?'

Tushar and Sukhbir recognize him instantly. He is the one who was brushing his teeth at the riverbank the day before Ganesh Chaturthi.

'Where's your toothbrush?' asks Sukhbir. Tushar bursts out laughing. So does the man. Others don't get the joke but don't mind joining them in a good laugh.

Within minutes, the prabhat pheri arrives at Ram Kund, where they find the professor and the purohit waiting. A man holding a large tray comes out of the famous sweet shop. He gives each person a small leaf-plate of srikhand one at a time.

'I have some news for you, Tushar,' says Professor Joshi. 'I met the municipal commissioner the other day. He showed great interest in the new water purification technology using proteins that I have been working on. He wants me to head the water filtration plant project, scheduled to begin next week.'

They now know what the srikhand is for. Tushar's reply to the professor is drowned in the sound of applause that follows.

The prabhat pheri moves on. When it reaches the road adjoining the Bhaji Bazaar, a woman in a sari draped in the traditional Marathi style approaches. Tushar and Aai know her well.

'Good to see you, Kaku,' says Aai to the usal woman. 'Good to see the young boy's love for the river, bai,' says the woman who sells usal. 'He is blessed by Tuka.'

BELOVED CITY

It is early winter now. The river sparkles in the soft morning light. It has been freed of water hyacinth. Quite a bit of concrete has also been dug out from the riverbed stretching from Ram Kund to Dutondya Maruti. There is a nip in the air, and it smells fresh.

Signs of change have begun to show.

The 8 a.m. sky dims when the clouds take over. The schoolboy's heart leaps away to the hilltops glimmering green in dreams. Daydreams. The feet moving toward school slow down. The backpack on the shoulders suddenly feels light. The face no longer has to work hard to stay calm.

The eleven-year-old's eleven-minute walk from home to school is a journey towards light. He can't count the rainbows that pour into his young head, but he knows he can count on them. Walking to school under a cloudy sky is a thrill that nothing can match. Little things like not having an umbrella hardly bother him. He does not miss what he does not have. The joy of approaching rain is a complete package in itself.

He can save time by hailing a bus across Ashok Talkies at Malegaon Stand or, if has gone on a bit further, opposite the Bank of Maharashtra near Indra Kund. There's no point in making the bus stop after he passes by the bank because it won't. Doesn't matter. The school is barely a four-minute walk from Panchvati Karanja.

Every day, just after he passes the paved ramp curving up from the left of the main road, a closed shop welcomes Tushar. A baby's face painted in black on the shutter smiles at him. It's the famous Murphy baby, Baba told him one day. In his mind, Tushar turns on the knob of a vintage Murphy radio, boxy yet elegant. He hears the baby giggle, its voice surrounded by the faint forest of static.

No melody in the world can drown out a baby's voice discovering itself in gushing gurgles, scattering the confetti of happiness on a morning when the sun hides behind clouds. Tushar loves the way the air feels and smells. He doesn't want the sun to come out. On a morning like this, all the light spreads from a baby's lips to the sky. On a morning like this, you don't need to walk to start a journey. A simple smile is enough to put you on a magic carpet.

When it is about to rain, how can you remain indoors? Tushar cannot resist the brownish-golden glow of the outdoors. He wants to see how his face looks in the puddles dotting the playground. He wants to feel the water caught in his shoes and the polka dots of mud spattered above the sock lines.

He wants to breathe in the humid air flowing through his beloved city.

GLOSSARY

Aai: Mother.
Baba: Father.
bala: Literally, 'my child'.
dabba ispies: A version of hide-and-seek. Here, 'dabba' means an empty metal or plastic container and 'ispies' means 'I spy'. In this game, the seeker guards a dabba placed inside a chalk circle on the ground. On spotting a hidden player, the seeker announces their name by banging the dabba on the ground. If anyone hiding sneaks up to the seeker without being noticed and kicks the dabba out of the circle, all the hiding players (spies) are declared free.
Dutondya Maruti: Literally, 'Two-Faced Maruti'. A huge idol of Hanuman depicting him in a unique pose on either side. It is a famous landmark near Ram Kund.
Kapaleshwar: Literally, 'Lord of the Skull'. A famous temple dedicated to Lord Shiva at Ram Kund. Kapaleshwar means 'Lord of the Skull'.
misal pav: A popular Maharashtrian street food with a spicy curry of usal and farsan (fried mixture of chickpea flour), served with a soft bun called pav. It is often garnished with chopped onions, coriander leaves, and a squeeze of lemon.
modak: A dumpling of rice flour dough filled with jaggery and grated coconut.
Paithani sari: A traditional handwoven silk sari named after the town of Paithan in Maharashtra.
Panchvati: Literally, 'the grove of five banyans'. Ram, Lakshman and Sita are believed to have lived there during their exile.
Ram Kund: A sacred bathing tank in Nasik where, according to popular belief, Lord Ram used to take a bath.
srikhand: A creamy Indian sweet made from strained curd, sugar, cardamom, and nuts.
usal: Legumes soaked in water and sprouted for one or two days. The legumes include sprouted matki, or moth beans, and sprouted moong beans. A small amount of soaked chickpeas, black-eyed beans, and peas is added to the mix.

ABOUT THE AUTHORS

'A Magical Yaosang': *Linthoi Ningthoujam*

Linthoi Ningthoujam was born in 1987 in Imphal, Manipur, where she lives with her family. She completed her higher studies at the University of Delhi, and she currently teaches literature to undergraduates. Her poems have been published in various anthologies and journals, including *Witness: The Red River Book of Poetry of Dissent* (2021), *The Bombay Literary Magazine* (2022) and the *Yearbook of Indian Poetry in English 2022* (2022). She loves long solitary nature-walks and strongly believes it enhances creativity. 'A Magical Yaosang' is her first attempt at fiction.

Acknowledgements

I am grateful to all who made my childhood memorable, to friends who showed me what it means to bond beyond familial ties and their little acts of love which meant the world to my younger self. I am thankful to my Ima and Baba, my first story-tellers; my Bachou, whose cupboard of comic books opened up a world of a different dimension; and Ningthou, my brother, for his encouragement.

This story would not have been possible without the constant love, support and active co-parenting of my partner, Herojit. I must also mention our child, Atiya, for always keeping me on my toes and inspiring parts of the story.

Natali Ningthoukhongjam, my poet-friend, thank you for always being there to read the roughest draft. I am also grateful to Gireesh Ningthemcha for his insights on the Halangkar and Brajamai traditions.

I would also like to extend my warmest thanks to Prerna Mathur of Scholastic India for believing in the synopsis, and to the whole team at Scholastic India.

'Something Borrowed': *Madhumita Gupta*

Madhumita is a writer/author who loves writing for children. She has written for most of the publications for kids in India. Writing for children gives her a legitimate reason and chance to get in touch with her inner child and live for that time being in a world of her own creation!

Born and brought up in Rajasthan, she is an educator who has been teaching since forever. It was as a teacher that she started seeing all kinds of characters in her students that went on to inspire her to write. Most of her students have made it to her stories!

Along with kid-lit, she has been writing for various national and international publications, notable among them are *Reader's Digest*, *The Times of India*, *Hindustan Times* and *India Currents*. She has been contributing humour, human interest stories and features on health, education and parenting. She has also written English textbooks for Macmillan's, Pearson's, and Mango

Publications. She took a break from teaching and writing to pursue a second Master's in 19th Century British Studies in English from the University of Nebraska-Lincoln (USA) in 2016. After her Master's she worked as a lecturer at the same university for three years.

Currently she divides times between writing and working as an Assistant Examiner at International Baccalaureate; a Teacher-Trainer / Resource Person for English Language Teaching with Oxford University Press, India and a Creative Writing Mentor with Scholastic, Asia.

When she's not reading, writing or teaching, she's most likely to be with her pet, Munnu, with whom she and her husband live in Rajasthan.

Acknowledgements

Writing is supposed to be a solitary activity but I have always felt that it takes a village to bring out a book! How one gets the germ of an idea, fleshes the story out, brainstorms all through it…till the point a book lands in the reader's hands, none of it could be done by just one person, or that's what I believe.

I owe 'Something Borrowed: Dida's Saris to the Rescue' first and foremost to my Dida, Ma, Mami, and Mashi whose vast collections of saris were the beginning of the idea.

Going in sequence about how the story got into its present shape, it was Nalini Sorenson who first read it and gave me the confidence that it could be submitted for publication. And then it was due to Loena Srivastava who encouraged me to submit it to Scholastic. I can't express how grateful I am to the editors at Scholastic – Ashley Kumar, Prerna Mathur, and Sakshi for their patience and guidance all along. I'd also like to thank Swati Sanyal Tarafdar for her 'Writing Together Sprint' which was just the shot I needed to complete this one!

And finally, there's no way I could have completed this book without my husband who kept me well-supplied with steaming cups of tea all through, as I sat huddled, writing furiously. And my son, who kept me buoyed up all through and critiqued the book whenever I needed those second, much sharper pair of eyes! And finally, Munnu, how could have I written this without your gentle brown eyes and wagging tail keeping me company!

'Godavari Days': *Sarabjeet Garcha*

Sarabjeet Garcha is a poet, editor, and translator. His five books of poems include *All We Have*, *A Clock in the Far Past*, and *Lullaby of the Ever-Returning*. He has also published a volume each of poems translated from Marathi and prose translated from Hindi. His translation of three long essays by the iconic Marathi playwright Mahesh Elkunchwar appeared as *The Necropolis Trilogy*.

He has translated several American poets into Hindi, including W.S. Merwin and John Haines, and several Indian poets into English, among them Mangalesh Dabral and Leeladhar Jagoori. His poems and translations have been published in the *Notre Dame Review*, *Versopolis*, *Lyrikline*, *Modern Poetry in Translation*, *Asymptote*, *Two Lines Journal*, *the Indian Quarterly*, *Scroll*, and *The Wire*, among other publications. He has also published essays and guest-edited special issues for poetry journals, the latest being the 2023 Indian Poetry Edition for *Verseville* (www.verseville.org). His poems have been featured in several anthologies, including *Yearbook of Indian Poetry in English*, *Modern English Poetry by Younger Indians*, and *Singing in the Dark*. He has read his poems at numerous national and international literary festivals.

Sarabjeet has received the Fellowship for Outstanding Artists from the Government of India, the International Publishing Fellowship from the British Council, and the inaugural Godyo Podyo Probondho Award. His poems have been translated into German, Spanish, Russian, Malayalam, Kannada, Marathi, Punjabi, and Hindi.

He is the founder and editorial director of Copper Coin (www.coppercoin.co.in), a multilingual publishing company based in Delhi NCR.

'Godavari Days' is his first story for children.

Acknowledgements

My nine-year-old twin sons, Amrit and Nimrat, often asked me if I could write a story for them. I promised I would, but never got round to actually doing it. Then, at the 2024 New Delhi World Book Fair, I ran into the bibliophile and ex-colleague Prerna Mathur. A few days later, when she asked me the same question, I was instantly reminded of Grand Master Oogway who, in the 2008 film *Kung Fu Panda*, says, 'There are no accidents.' Taking a cue from Master Oogway's faith in the unseen yet exacting powers of the universe, I readily said yes.

Thus began my exciting journey into the enchanting world of children's fiction, much to Amrit and Nimrat's delight. I had been looking for an effective means to share my fascination with the small city I grew up in and the river that runs through it. Prerna pointed out the way, for which I am immensely grateful. As managing editor, she provided invaluable support. Her expert handholding transformed the entire process, from initial concept to final draft, into a truly enjoyable experience.

A big thank you to Meera Menon, my first reader of everything I write for publication.

My heartfelt gratitude to Ashley Kumar for her meticulous scrutiny and judicious editorial suggestions.

I am also indebted to Bijal Vachharajani and Aditya Sharma for reading the final draft and offering useful comments.

Harsimran, my life companion, and Samardeep, my eldest son, can't be thanked enough for their endless love and constant encouragement.

Last but not least, a vigorous nod to Chandrima Chatterjee, without whose cheerful illustrations, the story wouldn't be what it is.